DOUBLE YOUR INCOME

8 Success Secrets From a Spectacular Life

CAROL M. PARIS

Double Your Income: 8 Success Secrets From a Spectacular Life
www.HomesInHawaii.com

ISBN-13:978-1981521104
ISBN-10:1981521100

Publisher
10-10-10 Publishing
Markham, ON
Canada

Printed in United States of America and Canada

TABLE OF CONTENTS

DEDICATION

To my parents, and my sons, Jeffrey, Ross, and William, and the other members of my immediate family, including Leslie, Amanda, and Jake.

ACKNOWLEDGEMENTS

TWA & United Flight Attendant Roommates:

Dori Hisle, Tommie Penn, Phyllis Pickell, Jan Thomasen, Cathlyn Clausen, Sarah Rehnard, Delores Del Cerro, and Ruth Eastlack.

The Cookhouse Café Crew and Friends:

Judy & Clay Wright, Delores Del Cerro, Liz Tonge, Loretta Boyle, "Cousin" Carol, Kris, Carmel, Danny, and Angela.

Dotty & Jim Walters, Marie & Fernando Gumucio, Brenda & Gordon Hepler, Lucille Biondi, Mary Carmozzi, Marie Dean, Barbara Lonick, and Larry Murphy.

Outstanding Agents at Carol Paris Brown, Inc:

Pam Canfield, Ross M. Brown and Jeffrey Parisse, Fredia Heppenstall, Sharon Slowik, Casie Quillin, Fran Kormann, David Norod, Phoebe Call, Joan Gordon, Bill Hardin, Elsie Smoluk, Nan Brent, Marjorie Barnard, Dean Gilbert, John Stacey, Vonnie Moeser, and Coleen Bagetta.

Keller Williams Honolulu colleagues:

Ross M. Brown, Jaime Reich, Supitcha Momsun, Cindy Cai, Colette Ching, Pamela Cleere, Theresa Fernandez, Diane Fujikami, Isabella Forster, Kristy Im, Adrienne Lally, Attilio Leonardi, Libby Lum, Kevin Miyama, Anthony Pace, Joe Paiki, John Stallings, and Ashliey Wasson.

I want to thank my family, friends, colleagues, and educators for being the inspiration for success, for my career and life purpose.

My brothers, Larry and Chuck Paris.

My sister-in-law Jill Paris, who is always in my court.

Dr. Robert Paris, my cousin and friend since day one.

Em Paris and Tony Paris, my amazing niece and nephew.

Shirley Hebert, Evelyn Milicia, Ken Sitkowski, Gene Sitkowski, Ed Cooper, Ray Quesada, Nancy Walrath, Don Deering, Dr. Murray Sachs, Cary Pollak, Madelyn Jennings, Howard Rooks, Ed Peete, Diane Large, Carole Di Quollo, Elaine Teachey, Nancy Spinks, Dori Jackson, Duffy and George Ftikas, Dr. William Erbe, Craig Buck, Gary Peterson, Brenda Shiplett, Adrienne Loughlin, Tracy Knepple, Mike Marketti, Lynn and Jerry Nelson, Bob Moulthrop, Debbie Cockrell, William A. Brown, Jim Warkentin, Judy Slack, Liz Ventrella, Michael Anastasia, Carol and Briggs Christie, Lynne and Bill Woods, Dr. Crossen, Mary Lou Wilkins, Eve Nichols, Taylor Le, MaryAnn O'Bara, Linda Baker, William Adam Brown, and Rachelle Joseph.

My Trainers:

Gary Keller, Tom Hopkins, Anthony Robbins, Howard Brinton, Jerry Rossi, Dick Dillingham, Ed Hatch, Bill Barrett, Rick Brown, Rick De Luca, Barb Schwarz, Pat Zaby, Gee Dunston, Bill Hardin, John Lane, Ed Gagle, Drexanne Evers, Danielle Kennedy, Mike Brody, Walter Sanford, Floyd Wickman, Brian Buffini, LeRoy Houser, Richard Flint, Dave Beson, and Brian Tracy.

A special thank you to Dean De Jesus, Judy Browning, Christina Cotten, and Raymond Aaron.

FOREWORD

Throughout this book, *Double Your Income: 8 Success Secrets From a Spectacular Life,* you will learn how Carol M. Paris seized opportunities, using her experiences to build her business and create financial growth. No matter where you are in your career or the development of your business, the lessons Carol shares will help you take the next step toward your goals.

You will be inspired by how Carol turned various changes in her life into opportunities, and she provides you with the secret keys to how she accomplished that. With each secret key, she gives you examples from her own experiences, including steps that you can follow to achieve success in your own business. Carol talks candidly about the obstacles she has dealt with, and you will be inspired by her positive mindset and determination to move forward.

Having met and talked with Carol, I was inspired, not only by what she was able to accomplish throughout her life, but by the circumstances she has overcome along the way. During a time in your life that you may be struggling to find a place in the workforce, she not only survived, but thrived! You will learn how to grow in your own life and get to know Carol and her amazing journey.

Raymond Aaron
New York Times Bestselling Author

ACCEPTING THE CHALLENGE TO DOUBLE YOUR INCOME

This day and age belongs to the entrepreneur. It is a time when businesses are being created at a rapid rate—some to explore a passion, some designed to build capital, and others to address global issues. You have an opportunity to try something new, and you may jump at it, inspired by the challenge and positive aspects of change.

Whatever the reason, you have decided to take the leap and join the world of entrepreneurs. Welcome! It is an exciting way to pursue your dreams, but this path also brings some unique challenges. Throughout my years in business, I have worked in sales, owned a restaurant, and created my own niche in relocation real estate. I have worked hard and strived, always looking for opportunities where others saw nothing at all.

My businesses have been successful and earned me a tidy income, allowing me to live a life that I love. But why have I been successful? I saw doors and windows of opportunity and challenges to explore, where others saw only walls and obstacles, choosing to give up or not take a risk.

It is this unique sense of vision that often sets entrepreneurs apart from others. We not only see what is, but we see possibilities and what can be. Not everyone has this vision. Some can only see the path laid out for them by someone else. They cannot see an alternative path or a different journey beyond the one already in front of them.

I did not see that traditional path as my future. Even though I started my career during a time when those who struck out on their own were often viewed with suspicion, I was determined to succeed. I also dealt with the boundaries set for women, which limited our opportunities and provided plenty of challenges.

Like so many women and men before me, I did not just accept what was. I created what I knew could be. And, I was successful, despite changing circumstances and the rhythm of life that could have bogged me down.

During all of these experiences, I faced a variety of challenges. But, I have found that 8 Success Secrets have kept me successful, no matter the circumstances or the industry. These are the secrets that I share in this book.

As an entrepreneur just starting out or one looking to grow along with your business, I will show you how I truly learned to bloom where I was planted.

My former husband's career took us throughout the United States of America, and we had the chance to live in a variety of climates and cultures. But, no matter where we were, I was looking for the opportunities available. I saw markets and potential, even as I juggled my family life and the demanding schedule dictated by my children's schooling, activities and general needs. I also did a great deal of entertaining for my husband's career. Keep in mind, that wasn't always easy.

My career started during a time where men were still seen as the primary breadwinner. Men routinely made more income, were offered better opportunities and were expected to be the full-time working spouse.

Throughout these chapters, I will talk about the different experiences in my life and how each of them helped me to grow, both as a person and as an entrepreneur. I saw areas and opportunities for growth, no matter the circumstances. How do you view your circumstances? Are they challenges that you can overcome or do you see them as insurmountable obstacles blocking your path?

Do not let the present-day circumstances or unexpected changes in your life stop you from achieving everything you want. There is no magic formula, but with the right mindset and the 8 Success Secrets, you can reach the level of success you desire in your life and business. So, let's get started!

WHAT DEFINES YOU?

Throughout my life, I have always been on the go. From a young age, I was looking for work and trying to do as many things as possible. My father used to worry that I wasn't enjoying *being a kid* because I always seemed to be rushing from one job or activity to another. But I loved the fast pace of my life then, and it has not changed into my adulthood.

Born in Ohio, I came from a blue-collar family. My father was a coal miner, but by the time I was four, my parents had decided to move to Detroit, Michigan. It was a bigger city with more work and more opportunities for our family. Not to mention, it was a better work environment than heading down into the mines. Many of the improved safety measures now in place to protect miners from the dangers involved, especially for their lungs, were not in place back then.

During my early years growing up in booming Detroit, it seemed the sky was the limit. Anything was possible if I was willing to work hard. The work ethic my parents showed me provided the inspiration to push forward and get things done, allowing me to enjoy the success of that effort.

My mother always said, "If you want a helping hand, look at the end of your sleeve." Her belief was not to whine but just keep moving. That was her philosophy in raising her three children. I am the eldest child.

My dad started out painting smokestacks for a factory, but eventually, he was hired into the steel industry. It was a great life in Detroit, at a time when the blue-collar family believed they were on top. Most people had plenty of everything, but nothing was extravagant. My goal back then was to live in a brick house. We lived in a wood frame house, but I thought the most exciting thing would be to live in a brick house, like all the rich kids.

I was always fascinated with houses, even way back then. At a certain point, I knew that I had to get out of Detroit to achieve some of my goals and also knew early on that I was going to be limited where I was. Going to the movies and seeing what California was like gave me the idea that I should move there and enjoy the sunshine and that exciting lifestyle. While Detroit was a great place to grow up at that time, the winters could be brutal.

To achieve what I wanted in life, I usually worked two or three part-time jobs. This included work at a men's clothing store and a drug store. My dad did not like this; it embarrassed him that I was always out working.

It all started when I was 10 or 11 years old, and I decided to shine shoes in my dad's friend's barbershop. When Dad found out, he came to the shop and told me to go home. That was the end of that job, but it wasn't the end of my entrepreneurial spirit!

Another opportunity I found was helping the local Avon® lady. I was still a kid, about 12 years old, but I quickly figured out a way to increase sales. I simply called on more customers. My first real part-time job was at a large bakery chain store called Awrey's Bakery® and I worked after school and on weekends. I was required to have a work permit and was able to obtain one since I was now 15 years old. They interviewed me and decided that I was best suited for sales, even though that is not what I applied for at the bakery. They gave me a small raise every week since I was outselling many of the full-time salespeople. Awrey's Bakery® offered me the opportunity to enter their management training program when I graduated high school. While this was a nice offer, I wanted to expand my knowledge and took a job at a physicians' clinic.

At 16 years old, I started working in an "industrial medical clinic" and people came in with pretty severe lacerations and other injuries. The doctors taught me to be calm and deal with emergencies. They also taught me to take X-rays, and I helped with the books if the bookkeeper couldn't make it in that day. Keep in mind; I was still in high school at the time.

Those doctors saw someone who was eager and willing to learn about everything. I was curious and worked hard. These qualities have never left me and are stepping stones to the success I achieve throughout my life.

Across the hall from the doctors' clinic was a local dentist, Dr. Sachs, who offered me a better position to help him open a dental office in another part of town. This was my first full-time job after graduating high school.

I became Dr. Sachs' office manager and helped him build up the practice from a one-chair to a four-chair practice. He taught me so many aspects of business in general, and how to work as a dental assistant. Now, I had not only medical experience but also dental.

My dad complained that I was always working too hard and needed to have more fun in life. At the time, I was looking to earn more money and travel, so I asked my parents for advice.

As a woman, my options were limited in the 1950s. Keep in mind, back then; blue-collar families rarely sent all their children to college. The boys went, and the girls started families or moved into the nursing or teaching professions. The funny thing was, I liked working better than school anyway, so I wasn't upset that my younger brothers were heading to college and I was not.

My father's suggestion was unique for the time, but it led me to see the world. He suggested that I become a flight attendant with the airlines. Back then, this was a job with prestige and was considered a key part of the luxury of flying. My mother, who said my head had always been in the clouds, agreed it would be a good job for me. I was 20 years old.

Trans World Airlines, known as TWA, was running an ad looking for flight attendants and they held interviews in Detroit. So, I took a couple of hours off and went down to interview for the flight attendant position. At that time, they only chose one out of every 50 applicants. The odds were not in my favor. It was competitive because their standards were extremely high, yet I was called for a second interview. TWA requested that I come to their headquarters in Kansas City, Missouri, and they sent me a plane ticket.

That was my first airplane flight. No one in my family had ever flown before, and this experience was something I could have never imagined. I can still remember what I wore as I boarded the plane. When I arrived in Chicago for my connecting flight, I waited in the lobby along with another young lady who was also interviewing with TWA.

The plane did not depart, and eventually, I said to myself, something is wrong here. Wanting to figure out what happened, I went to the desk. I told the woman that the flight was supposed to leave 30 minutes ago. She laughed and said that the flight had left on time, but I had missed it because I was sitting in the lobby and not by the gate. That was the beginning of my airline work.

She did find us another flight, and we made it to the interview. We then joined approximately 100 young ladies in this large room where we were kept waiting for most of the day. Later on, I realized they were observing us to see how we did when we were forced just to sit around and wait. It was a skill that came in handy because we were often waiting as flight attendants or hostesses as they used to call us at TWA. We would be waiting for a plane or waiting because of an engine problem. The list could go on, but through all of that, we had to be patient and still provide a wonderful experience for our passengers.

Needless to say, during that inspection, the girls who handled themselves well, demonstrated a good deal of patience, and socialized well with the others seemed to be the ones that were hired. I know there were women there with more education than I had who seemed like better candidates, but they did not get hired. I am extremely patient, however, and I did get hired.

When you try something new, you might not succeed at first, but do not assume that the answer will always be no. Like my flight attendant interview process, sometimes the answer turns out to be yes!

It was one of the best jobs that I could ever have. I traveled everywhere, and we were treated like movies stars. It was a great life! I was transferred to San Francisco, California, where I lived with six other young women in a three-story Pacific Heights mansion. It was a fantastic time in my life, and I enjoyed it immensely.

That job gave me the chance to travel extensively, and travel became a significant part of my life, even after I was no longer a flight attendant. Over the years, I have traveled to 46 states, including Alaska, and also Canada, Bermuda, the Caribbean, Mexico, Central America, United Kingdom, Europe (all over), Turkey, Greece, Australia, New Zealand, the South Pacific, Japan, China, and other wonderful places.

In San Francisco, I met my former husband. We married there and were soon transferred to Stockton, California, for his work. I was still flying at that time but eventually left the airlines. We knew that another transfer for his career was imminent. My long car commutes back and forth to the San Francisco airport, before and after my coast to coast, eight-hour flights, were taking a toll on me. Free cigarettes were given out on the food trays during flights. Remember, passenger cigarette smoking, not cigars or pipes, was allowed during airline flights at that time. All of this adversely affected my health and I left the airlines.

We then moved to Sacramento, California. There I joined the Pacific Bell Telephone Company and became the first woman to sell their commercial equipment to businesses in the area. I was one saleswoman with 30 salesmen. That was in 1960 and, let me tell you; it was a different work environment than today. I couldn't go into the storeroom without getting pinched or lean over my desk without getting patted. Having worked in the airlines for years, I could manage it. The men definitely gave me a rough time, but the tougher time came from the women in that office. There were no other women in my department, but they were scattered throughout the company. Here I was, this young bride walking into a plum job that they had all missed out on for some reason. I was definitely feeling the dislike coming my way, and I often went home crying.

About that time, International Business Machines – IBM, called me. I had interviewed with them also, and they offered me a position in staff support, which I took. I worked for them for several years and enjoyed it. They were a wonderful company to work for, but my manager wanted to hire my husband away from his employer at the time and get him to sell for IBM.

In those years, a husband and wife couldn't both work for IBM in the same office. It was against IBM policy. We knew that the greater career was going to be his and not mine, even though I helped make sales for some of the salesmen. There just were not any sales positions for women there at this time.

It was time to start a family; I stepped aside and stayed at home. I gave up my position, and my husband began working for IBM. That was the beginning of my life of relocations. The joke with people who work for IBM is that the letters stand for "I've Been Moved." Each of my children were born in different states as we relocated for my husband's career. From the West Coast to the East Coast, we saw a wide variety of the United States.

After my third son was born, we were transferred from Connecticut to Kailua, Oahu, Hawaii, for three years. This is where I first fell in love with island living and have owned a home in Kailua since 1968. In 1971, we were again transferred by IBM to California and the San Francisco "Bay Area." It was nice to be close to my in-laws again because it gave my boys a chance to get to know their relatives including their grandparents. This was where I opened my restaurant. It was one of the most fun things that I have ever done.

I started out with a partner, Judy Wright, and we opened the restaurant on an old ranch. We were located in what used to be the cookhouse. It was a great success! We changed the menu nearly every day. We took advantage of the ranch setting and used it as a theme throughout the restaurant—from the denim on the walls to the chaps made of gingham that served as aprons. Unique shops also opened in the same building, including Larry Murphy Pottery, antiques, gift boutiques, and a flower shop.

For additional income, we were even selling some of the restaurant's antique tables and chairs. We had to stop because it took too long to replace the items we were buying in San Francisco.

My family and I made a huge commitment to see this project through because we could see that it was going to be a big success. I ended up expanding the restaurant from just a few tables to over 20 tables. It was the "in place" for people to go, even the mayor. We were a hit in this small community.

Now what makes this even more unique is that we did not get financing from our husbands. They said, if we wanted to do this, we were on our own. Two banks turned us down; then, one of the bankers suggested we go across the street to Security Pacific Bank. "Those nutty women would love this," he said. These women dressed up on Fridays in western garb, similar to pioneer women's dresses. The women were just delightful.

Judy and I went to them and shared our plan. We explained that we would be the first natural food, full-service restaurant with locally grown produce from our area. We were also not going to allow smoking in the restaurant. A non-smoking restaurant was unusual for that time period, even for California. We feared that people may not come to a non-smoking restaurant. The bankers asked us to sit down, and they said we would have to do a *pro forma*. I did not have a clue what they were talking about at the time. The women at the bank helped us to fill out the paperwork, and we ended up borrowing $12,000 to outfit The Cookhouse. The original cookhouse had the major appliances and dishes in place, so we only had to add to it, hence the reason that we borrowed so little.

We took the restaurant's name from its former use, calling it The Cookhouse Café, which was part of the old Moraga Ranch. We opened on March 4th, 1975.

Our creative idea ended up with a line of people that started at 10:00 am and did not end until 4:00 pm each afternoon. We turned the tables at the restaurant at least four times a day. Keep in mind; we were only open for brunch and lunch!

We found out that a student attending Stanford University's School of Business suggested that our restaurant model is what they should be studying since it encompassed all the principles being covered in their business course. My financial numbers and the popularity of the restaurant, which is still in business today, proves that it is definitely a model to follow.

Training your staff is critical to the success of your business. My restaurant had ten employees, plus independent contractors and summer help, who needed my supervision. One of the new summer staff was observed pouring unused wine from glasses back into the carafe as she cleared tables. That same employee owned a horse and was asking customers to give her the leftovers from their meal for her horse. Needless to say, she was retrained in a hurry. Never assume your employees have the same level of standards that you do.

My partner left after a few months because it was too much of an obligation for her. We had planned to each work only three days a week—how naïve! After a period of time, with my partner having left the business, I realized that I needed to either give it up or expand. After talking with my family, we decided to expand by opening an outdoor patio with ten umbrella tables. Later, we decided to open a second restaurant in a neighboring town, as well as to market my original salad dressings and a cookbook. Just when that decision was made, we were transferred again!

I ended up selling the restaurant for a nice profit, and it remains successful for the current owners under a different name. This was my first taste of success as a business owner, but it was not to be my last. I worked as a travel agent for a short period of time while living in Boulder, Colorado, which was a natural shift for me since I used to be a flight attendant.

Eventually, we settled in Virginia. After all these moves, it was here that I had a friend suggest that I enter the real estate business. At first, I hesitated, but I eventually studied for the exam and earned my real estate license. We were close to the military bases and government offices in Northern Virginia; many of the real estate agents in the area focused on the military and government employees as their primary market.

Now, at the time, I did not know much about military or government employees but, after numerous transfers, I knew about corporate moves and relocation. This is truly a business within a business. You are dealing with corporations, the transferees, and the trauma of children being moved from their friends and schools. Teenagers would have to leave boyfriends, girlfriends, and their grandparents; the emotions involved can be difficult. Single people may also have challenges relocating because they don't have another person to validate their choices. A highly skilled agent can help inform these people, so they can make clearer decisions.

Some scoffed at the idea and told me that no one would know what I was talking about when I mentioned "Relocation." I was confident that I knew what I was talking about and decided that I was going to pursue it, no matter what.

Around that time, I attended a local Chamber of Commerce meeting where I met a woman whose husband was in real estate. She told me that he receives requests from clients for help with residential real estate, but he preferred commercial real estate. She suggested that I take over that aspect of the business for him. I agreed to do what I could.

I also learned that the newspaper *USA Today*® owned by Gannett Company, Inc. was locating to our area. So, I called the woman in charge of the Human

Resources Department—Diane Large—and invited her to lunch. Fortunately, she agreed. At lunch, I learned that she was from the same area in California where I had owned my restaurant. In fact, Diane had been one of the regulars and lived in the neighborhood!

She confirmed they were starting a new paper and asked for my help with their short-term renters. Now, in the real estate business, there is little money to be made with renters, but I saw an opportunity to grow my business. I told her that I would assist and, for months, worked without pay helping to get these renters settled.

The Human Resources Department remembered me, thanks to my seminars helping the renters to become accustomed to the area. Once the buyers started coming in, they gave me the chance to work with these relocating employees. Now, at last, there was an opportunity for me to earn real income. I then provided buying seminars to assist the transferees. These people were moving from many different places to Northern Virginia and the Washington, D.C. area. It was a significant cultural change for some of them.

The parent company, Gannett Company, Inc., decided to move their headquarters from Rochester, New York, to Northern Virginia. The Human Resource Department referred these transferees to me. Madeline Jennings, Senior Vice-President of Personnel at Gannett, was a huge part of these referrals to my business. Gannett flew me to New York on several occasions to meet with the spouses of the transferees and to hold seminars about their upcoming relocation.

Then, Mobil Oil, who later merged with Exxon, moved their headquarters to Fairfax, Virginia. I was referred their business as well and flew to New York City to meet their management. I wanted to see how I could assist them with the transferring of their employees and handled over 60 of their transferees. I was repeatedly contacted by these, and many other companies, as they transitioned their employees to new offices and headquarters. These buyer transferees later turned into sellers of real estate.

The amount of work that came from these connections eventually led me to open my own company, Carol Paris Brown, Inc. I couldn’t keep up with everything on my own and needed help to meet the demand.

My income kept doubling after that as I continued to get business from other companies relocating to the area. I did not look for the paycheck, however. I have learned that the paycheck comes if you do a good job. With a corporation, if you mess up with one transferee, the chain is broken, and that is the end of it. Complaints are not tolerated.

My business is all about service, and everything I do is about making it more comfortable for the transferees. I am determined to assist them, finding hotels for their stay while we search for their next home and helping them become familiar with the area. I take these people to dinner, send them flowers and fruit baskets, and help them with any other details that they might need.

This includes assisting them in finding an agent to sell their current property in another state and replacements for services they had in their previous location.

The parents received Relocation Kits with information about the Washington, D.C. and Northern Virginia area. I decided to create a similar one for the kids, including information about the local fun restaurants, parks, and other places that appeal to children. I sent these via FedEx® to the family and included small gifts, helping them to get excited about moving to their new hometown. The idea was to make it more comfortable for the junior members of the family. If you make the children happy, then you find the parents are more willing to work with you.

My success showed that I was good at building a quality level of customer service for each of my clients. I worked with a great team at my company, and our success demonstrated that we were each giving our best to our clients.

It was a golden time, and I decided that I could add a construction component to my business. I sat at my desk one morning and prayed that a builder would come into my life. That afternoon, Ed Peete of Arlington, Virginia, was referred to me by another builder and Ed came to my office. He was just starting out his building career. Ed Peete Company built around 100 homes during a 14-year period. Ed had me list and sell all of these properties for his firm during the years we worked together.

When I moved back to Hawaii, I asked Ed to write a letter of recommendation for me. He said, *"Carol, just tell them that #1, you always got my price, and #2, you never upset our customers. That is all they need to know. You're great!"* My work with him included many hours selecting the names of homes, choosing floor plans, cabinets, flooring materials, paint colors, brochure details, and conducting the sales themselves. I was truly involved in all aspects of the business. This knowledge served as an asset for my other clients since I was a resource for these individuals as well.

Eventually, I sold this thriving business and returned to Hawaii, where I have continued to work and receive sales awards in real estate. The 8 Success Secrets have been part of my life, regardless of what business I have been involved with at the time.

These are the experiences that defined me and make me the successful businesswoman that I am today. What defines you? What experiences have helped to mold you into jumping into the world of entrepreneurship and owning your own business?

Take a minute to list just a few of those moments. They are what define you and determine how you interact with others. Getting to know yourself is critical to moving forward professionally and personally. If you do not know who you are, it will be hard to put the 8 Success Secrets to work effectively.

Throughout the following chapters, I am going to share these secrets with you and how they impact my businesses. These 8 Success Secrets are the action items you need to take your business and career to the next level!

Success Secret #1

Quality – Your Reputation is Your Brand

When you think about a career as an employee, who would you say is the client? Many of you would probably say the employer, and you would be right. When you are on the job, it is important to provide high-quality in your work in all the tasks you are assigned. Staying focused and on task are part of that level of quality. Doing so allows you to be in a position to take advantage of opportunities when they present themselves to the company.

During my entire working career, I built a great reputation with all my employers. It meant that they were able to provide a reference for me later in my career even though I did not work in the same industry. Why?

Your reputation is your brand. If you take the time to build a high-quality brand, it will benefit you and your business in the long run, both in terms of suppliers and clients. Even if those individuals are outside of your main industry, their recommendations and support will serve your business well when building your client base.

As an entrepreneur, making quality part of how you perform all your work is even more critical to your success than it is as an employee.

Quality also comes into play in terms of the type of product or service you provide. When you make sure that every client receives the highest quality from your business, it translates into satisfied clients, and those are the ones who return. Your success, no matter what the industry, will be based on drawing in and keeping a repeat clientele.

One of my best experiences with quality was in my restaurant. When my husband's job relocated us yet again, I decided, with the kids in school, that I should start a business. Partnering with another mom to open a restaurant entailed a certain level of risk.

However, we were ahead of our time in many ways. For example, we decided to use homemade recipes that catered to our unique local crowd. This also meant that we sourced most of our ingredients locally as well. The quality of our offerings appealed to our clientele, and they kept coming back. We were busy with a brunch and lunch crowd consistently. Outperforming the chain restaurants was about providing something they could not: a unique local experience. We were not looking to beat them at their own game because we did not want to play that game. We just wanted to be the very best at what we were trying to create, local, fresh food in a charming and unique, smoke-free environment.

What about your business? Are you a small player in a larger industry that is dominated by some big brands? Instead of trying to provide the exact same offerings as the big guys, why not look for the products or services they are missing? Competing head to head might not be your best route. Sometimes the best route may be to create your own niche (more about that later).

When I opened my restaurant, I knew some of the risks involved and the realities of the industry. Most restaurants fail within the first two years. The overhead costs can be significant, and the profit margins are often rather thin. This is a business where repeat clients are critical, and having a menu that draws people in is as important as the attitude of your staff. Even the best restaurants fail when they do not make a connection with their community.

Yet despite this knowledge, I moved forward. Why? Because I knew I had something of high-quality to offer my community. I wanted to give my new business a chance to grow and succeed; my strong belief meant that I was willing to work and overcome the odds.

Understand this: You need to know what the potential risks are when starting out in your industry of choice. But do not let that scare you from getting started. Instead, let that knowledge guide you to avoid pitfalls, which could sink your business before it even gets off the ground.

There are a lot of hazards inherent to the restaurant business, especially when you are new to the business model like we were. Our employees were relying on us to build a business that would provide a livelihood for them as well, and not just for a short period of time. It was a lot of pressure to get it right for all of us.

We were in charge of creating something that would bring people back for brunch and lunch on a regular basis. It meant training our staff to provide a quality product with superior service, every time, for every customer. That focus on quality paid off in the end. After we were open for a relatively short time, we were profitable. Hiccups did not deter us; they were just a chance for us to get better, and that is what we did.

Here, we were exceeding expectations, including our own. The clientele was so loyal that we quickly grew our number of regulars. Customers also clamored for us to open for dinner, which would have added another shift for us. The temptation was there; I have to admit. We were already profitable, so that would have been gravy on top. But my partner and I had to weigh the costs.

Those costs were significant. We both would have been forced to reduce our family time; we would have needed to be away from our families during dinner and those early evening hours. It would have meant missing those routines we both enjoyed, including time with our children, checking in with everyone's day, and even the bedtime routines. As wives and mothers who truly enjoyed this time with our families, it was a sacrifice we were unwilling to make.

Plus, there was the concern for the quality of the product coming out of the restaurant. When you begin to grow, there is a chance that your standards can start to slip. To avoid this, it is important to manage your growth and not let it get ahead of you, putting you and your business in over your head.

Our restaurant was a big part of our lives; we essentially put our names on every dish coming out of that kitchen. As part of that, one of us was always at the restaurant during the hours of operation. Problems could be quickly resolved because we were present. As an owner of a business in its infancy, I found the need to be hands-on to ensure that the product produced met my standards consistently.

As an entrepreneur, it is important to recognize that a new business of any kind is going to demand a significant chunk of your time and attention. If you want to train a staff to produce a product or service at a specific level of quality, then you need to lead the way. But it is more than just being present to bark orders. It means getting your hands dirty when production falls behind, or you see potential bottlenecks so that what your client receives doesn't fall below your level of quality just to meet a deadline. Your willingness to get in there with your staff sets the standard for your business and creates a level of expectation that your employees will then strive to meet on a daily basis with each customer or client.

Remember, your reputation and that of your business rides on every interaction your clients have with your services and products. A mediocre experience can often register as negative for a client, simply because they were not thrilled or left not feeling truly satisfied with the overall experience.

When I first obtained my real estate license, I also worked as marketing director for Champions Unlimited in the Washington, D.C. Metro area, including Northern Virginia and Maryland. The company was owned by Tom Hopkins, who was a top real estate salesperson and trainer. Today, he is a well-known, international teaching guru and author for business training. Tom has written, as of today, nineteen books, including *How to Master the Art of Selling.* Tom Hopkins has had over five million people, on five continents, attend his high-energy sales seminars. I sold seminars and products for his business and witnessed his sales training. Tom taught others to maximize their sales capabilities. The training I heard during those events in 1978 gave me the confidence to build my own *spectacular* real estate career.

After I left Champions Unlimited, I continued working in real estate and quickly became one of the top salespeople in my office. During that time, I met a wonderful woman named Pam Canfield. She worked as a Relocation Coordinator in our Relocation Department. Pam was an asset in terms of working with clients, managing the big picture, and all the details necessary to keep any business running smoothly.

The owner-broker hired a new Relocation Director, who decided to bring in her own people. This meant that Pam was let go. I was so incensed at what seemed patently unfair that I told Pam we were going to start our own relocation business. We marched downtown and bought our first box of office supplies. It quickly became apparent that I needed to sell even more homes in order to keep our business afloat in those early months.

Pam Canfield's work was essential for the growth of my company, Carol Paris Brown, Inc.; she became the Relocation Director of our relocation referral company, one of eventually six divisions. For the 14 years that we worked together, Pam and I never had a fight. We were a great team, and when I sold the company, she stayed on for a few more years with that firm.

In many areas of my real estate career, I was fortunate enough to work with quality people who knew their areas of expertise and gave their jobs 100% of their effort. The results were evident in our sales numbers and the bottom line of these businesses.

Carol Paris Brown, Inc. was founded in 1986 and eventually grew to serve several markets within the real estate industry. I saw opportunities to create divisions in my company to meet specific needs. One division was directed towards those with special needs. Many homes have multiple floors and a lot of stairs. These homes rarely came with elevators, and not everyone wanted that kind of floor plan. Those with special needs might need an alternative floor plan if that is what they wanted. I hired a registered nurse with a real estate license, Joan Gordon, and she headed up this division for me; it helped define our company as unique. Joan did a great job.

Another division was New Homes, where I worked with builders to sell the new homes in their developments. One of my sons, Ross M. Brown, R was instrumental in helping me coordinate this division. There was Property Management for rentals and, of course, my Relocation division. All of these areas contributed to the success of my business, and my staff was rewarded for providing quality service every time. They were invested in the success of my business, and my success was directly related to how well these agents did their jobs and the experiences they provided to customers and clients.

In total, we had six divisions: General Brokerage, Relocation, New Homes, Special Needs, Commercial Real Estate, and Property Management. David Norod was not one of my agents but came to me one day and said that he wanted to start a property management division with me. I knew David would provide quality service to the public and gave him the go-ahead to join my company and start this division. Our Property Management division turned out to be a decision that was profitable for everyone. When you have a reputation of quality, honesty, and ethics, you become a magnet for people who want to work with you.

When I sold the company, I sold David all of the property management accounts. He is still in business today. Working with David Norod was another opportunity that presented itself to me; he built this part of the business from the ground up and was key to the success of this division.

During my time in real estate, it became apparent that quality is best defined by the type of service you offer to your clients, including how accessible you are to answer questions and your overall responsiveness. When I book a client to show property, I give them the entire day. I do not want them to feel rushed through the process because of having to keep to a specific schedule.

Instead, I want clients to focus on finding the best home for them. They need to be able to walk through the homes, looking at the details that will play a part in their everyday lives. Does the space work for them? Can they imagine themselves in it during their daily lives or at special moments, like graduations, birthdays or anniversary celebrations?

This is clearly a process that requires clients to imagine and envision themselves in a space, something they can't do if they are rushed. It is important that everyone feels comfortable, therefore making the transfer less traumatic.

Most of these relocations are taking families away from everything that is familiar. When they are looking for a new property, they are trying to recreate a home for their immediate family. It is a process that cannot be rushed. You want them to be excited about their new home, not feeling as if they just settled for a house that was available in order to complete the process.

A family that feels rushed into making a decision is not likely to be happy with the result. This will translate into the number of referrals, or lack of referrals, that they send your way.

As an entrepreneur starting a new business, part of the quality that you offer is in the experience that you create for your clients. If they feel rushed, or feel as if they are just a number, then you are likely to lose their business. Making them feel special, like they are your only client, is crucial to creating that quality experience for them.

How do you make sure you are meeting your client's expectations? You need to really understand what they expect, and make sure that the quality of your products and services meet those expectations. Once you do, then the amazing experience will be possible, and it can happen with every client.

However, you cannot just guess at what they want and hope you have it right. You have to know. And that leads me to the second secret of my success…

Success Secret #2

Give the People What *They* Want

When it comes to real estate or any business, it is critical to remember that people are not going to use a service or buy a product that doesn't give them value while addressing their wants and needs.

This is especially true when it comes to real estate. I have conducted plenty of house showings where the family has big dreams but a limited budget. It is my job to find a home that they can get excited about within their price range.

As a real estate agent, my job is to focus on how I can address their needs and their wants. It means taking the time to really listen to my clients and find out how they live, not just what they want. Once you factor in budgets, then the choice is often made for them, but you still have to give them all the options.

When I start showing them properties, I make sure to note what speaks to the clients and what turns them off about a property. You would be amazed at how many clients give me a laundry list of wants, but when I show properties that match those wants, it quickly becomes apparent that those wants do not match their lifestyle. I must dig deeper at times because I need to find out what they really want, not just the surface items on a list.

No matter what your business, it is important not only to listen to what your client wants but also to focus on what they really need. You will be surprised at how often the two do not necessarily line up together. It is your job to find a way to make those two areas meet in the middle so that you have a satisfied client who is likely to recommend you to others.

You may also find yourself needing to decipher their unspoken wants. These are the things they might not acknowledge or even recognize that they want, but clearly, are going to factor into their satisfaction level with your services or products. Once you identify them, then you can go about meeting these expectations or wants, therefore giving your client the quality of service you wish them to receive.

The question is how to address those disconnects when a client is not happy about their situation, or their wants list exceeds their financial limitations. The key is often to turn their thoughts away from what doesn't work in a property and, instead, get them focused on what does work. This could also mean giving them potential solutions for addressing parts of the home that might not work for them at the moment. With a little imagination, clients can warm up to a property that might not have initially caught their fancy.

Granted, it is still an uphill battle to find the perfect property. The reason is that no property offers everything a client wants. As the real estate agent, it is critical to meet at least 80% of their expectations and give them solutions for the other 20%. In this way, you are addressing all their wants and needs, while at the same time recognizing that no property is perfect.

In your business or industry, your clients may also face limitations which impact the types of services they can afford. You may need to also refocus them on what works, instead of allowing them to dwell on what they cannot afford or what doesn't fulfill their initial expectations. When you turn them from the negative to the positive, it is a connection that will likely bring them back to your business.

Walking a client through a home, I am always watching for their reactions and their objections. One of the main things that I cannot change about a property is its location. So, I focus on that first and foremost. But how do you find the right location for your client?

I am constantly asking questions about the client's lifestyle, what they like to do, and how they spend their free time. It's also good to get an idea of their school needs if they have children, and where the parents are going to be working. As you can see, I am always collecting specific information about what they want, even when the conversation seems to be about casual topics.

In your business, getting to know your client can help you get on the right track to meeting their needs and wants. Note how I am always asking specific questions. This assists in drawing them out to speak openly with me. Not everyone you meet is eager to share information about themselves or their families. Still, I do not know anyone who doesn't enjoy talking about themselves if you appear genuinely interested and willing to listen. Well-framed questions can show the client you are interested and get them to open up with you.

However, as a real estate professional, there are also moments when you might find yourself having to give your client news they do not want to hear, or that can be very disappointing. In your line of work, have you had to be the bearer of bad news? It can be an awkward situation and will require all your finesse to salvage something for your client and your business.

For instance, there is a reality for my clients that I do not always enjoy sharing. They are often going to have to make some hard choices about location. In Hawaii, most activities are based outdoors, including on the beach. It seems that almost every client moving to the islands wants a house on the beach, close to great restaurants and shopping but also with plenty of living space. In Hawaii, it is impossible to get that in everyone's price range. It may be a pie in the sky dream for some, but one that still is the basis of many wish lists.

I sometimes have to burst that bubble, but I want to do it gently. I usually am able to get them a home close to the beach rather than on the beach, so that they can still participate in the water-based activities they enjoy.

In your business or industry, you might not be required to get to know your clients as personally as I do. But, if you are going to get them excited about a service or product that you are offering, then it is up to you to make sure you know what they want, and meet those expectations if possible.

If you cannot, then you should get as close as possible, and be able to offer solutions that address the areas where you are not able to provide exactly what they want or need. Remember, these solutions are a value-added part of your business and one that shouldn't be ignored. Where a client sees value, they often return to do business again, bringing others with them.

The reality of any business is that dissatisfied customers are always more vocal than those who are satisfied. These days, the dissatisfied do not just tell their friends about their experience; they get on social media and spread the story to millions of your potential clients. Your brand and reputation take a hit as a result. There are plenty of ways to address these dissatisfied clients after the fact. The reality is, at that point, you are doing damage control, which is reactionary. You may only have limited results in repairing your damaged brand's reputation.

The time to be proactive is when the client is right in front of you. Take them from being a dissatisfied or unhappy client to one who is excited to be working with you. Make them feel that they are being heard and that you are trying to meet their wants and needs. Listening is the key part of how you find out what your client expects and allows you to gauge their willingness to compromise.

It is also vital to understand how your clients are receiving your product or service. In my restaurant, we were constantly evaluating the menu and listening to feedback. When an item on the menu was panned, we tried to adjust it to meet the expectations of our customers. Sometimes, we simply changed some of the ingredients and the name of the dish and then people loved it! But, if that wasn't possible, we simply had to acknowledge that this item had to be removed from the menu.

Your loyalty to a product or service that is not helping your company reach the next level is counterproductive and a waste of valuable capital and resources.

If I had hung on to menu items that were not selling well, then I would have been sinking capital into ingredients and tying it up in a way that wouldn't have realized a return on our expenses. The overhead of a restaurant can be extremely high. So, the menu should always be subject to adjustment. This is true of any business.

No service or product should be considered truly indispensable. Recognize that little is truly basic and fundamental to your business offerings, and adjustments are crucial to a healthy bottom line. Give the people what *they* want.

Here is where feedback becomes critical. Keep in mind; there are two types of feedback: positive and negative. You and I both enjoy positive feedback because it usually results in more money, more praise, and more satisfied clients.

Negative feedback, however, is not usually greeted with the same enthusiasm, even though it can actually be the more powerful of the two. Why? Because negative feedback can provide useful data about how you are doing in your business. It is the best way to find opportunities to improve. It is a place where you can grow, allowing you to get even closer to reaching your goals.

The restaurant taught me that it is important to be flexible in the number of offerings available. Quality can be difficult to maintain when you have too many options at the same time. Growth is important to any business, but if a portion of your business is no longer contributing to your growth, and even draining resources from other profitable zones, consider adjusting your offerings to cut the dead weight.

If you have expanded too quickly, you might be offering services that are limiting the available resources needed for client favorites or be reducing the overall quality of your business services. Your employees might feel frazzled and overwhelmed, which also impacts the experience of your clients.

Finding out your client's needs, and then meeting them, might include focusing your business more narrowly versus being too broad in your services and products. Doing a few things well that your clients can count on is a better path to success than one that is built on providing multiple offerings, but with only so-so quality.

Think back to an experience you had with a company that provided multiple services or products in a specific industry. What was it like dealing with them?

Did the staff seem overworked because they had too many things going at the same time? Did they seem overwhelmed by the offerings in which they had to be knowledgeable?

If you are choosing to grow, then make sure that the growth path works for your business. Be prepared with the right training for your employees and schedule follow-ups with them to learn about their experiences. It is this feedback that can help you to determine if your training modules need to be tweaked or if they are effective. When employees feel you are invested in them, then they provide the best quality service for your clients consistently.

Feedback from employees is critical to reaching your goals more quickly. Responding to feedback helps you to find out where you are veering off course; thus allowing you to make corrections to address your business' needs. If you do it often enough, your business will meet and then exceed your expectations.

Avoid responding to feedback by getting mad or ignoring it. When you do so, you are missing out on an evaluation that could transform your business and take it to the next level. Remember, feedback is information. It is not a personal attack on you or your business. Ignoring feedback only limits the potential of your business. It doesn't hurt the other person if you choose to push this information away from you; it hurts you.

When employees give you feedback, make sure they know that it is welcomed. Making it uncomfortable to give feedback is likely going to mean your employees will just keep their mouths closed. This could mean that you miss a great opportunity or fail to notice a potential problem that negatively impacts your clients. Being on the front lines, your employees have a different perspective of your business, and that perspective deserves to be heard.

Corrective feedback gives you the ability to make changes. You cannot fix what you do not know is broken. Always be willing to ask for feedback, no matter what the situation, and be open to what you receive. When you know a client or employee is dissatisfied, you also need to know what will satisfy them, in detail. Essentially, what can your company do to create a winning product or service that will leave your client satisfied, and your employee excited to be part of the team?

Feedback doesn't always come from nice little surveys sent by a marketing team. It comes in a variety of ways from your employees and your clients. It could be a quick conversation in the break room, or part of a meeting with a client to discuss the next steps in their project. No matter how it is offered, you need to be open to receiving it.

When you take the time to listen, it can open up possibilities you did not even realize were there. The point is to not only do it better next time but make sure there is a next time with your clients.

As you can see, a willingness to learn from feedback can lead to constant improvement. None of us are perfect. I can find areas where I have made mistakes in my life. But what I have always done is commit to improving.

It doesn't mean I always make gigantic leaps, but I focus on small changes done consistently over time. Those small changes then turn into big changes, both for my personal and professional life.

Be committed to making changes in your business with the goal of constantly improving the process. When you do, you will reach your goals faster and with more consistency, which will shine through to your clients and your employees.

In this way, your clients get exactly what *they* want, every time they do business with you!

Success Secret #3

Create Your Own Niche

After a number of relocations for my former husband's career, we ended up on the East Coast. During my time there, I was able to enter the real estate market by getting my license and starting to grow my business. I was also keeping my antenna up for new opportunities. Never assume you are at the top of your game. Acknowledge that improvement is possible, even within an established industry. Within real estate, I found the underserved relocation market.

Many of the larger companies coming into my area were looking to relocate employees. The employees were left on their own to do several things. They had to buy a new home, sell their old house, and get their belongings transferred to the new home, all in time to report to work within the assigned timeframe. As you can see, it can quickly become an overwhelming process.

For companies, quality employees are worth their weight in gold. These are the employees who can assist your company in growing and reaching short and long-term goals, particularly if you are looking to expand beyond your current market. When opening a new site or attempting to boost the sales or productivity of a new location, it is a wise idea to relocate seasoned employees. They have the knowledge of your products and services, along with a commitment to provide quality.

If you are relocating your corporate headquarters then a large number of staff, including support personnel, will need to be relocated. These individuals will be pulling up stakes and coming to a whole new area, with a new culture to assimilate as well. I remember speaking to New Yorkers about relocating to the Washington, D.C. area and it was an eye-opener for them. Things are definitely not done the same way in the "Big Apple" as they are in Northern Virginia, the District of Columbia, and Maryland. As an example, one corporation offered driving lessons as part of the relocation for those New Yorkers who had always used subways and had never before driven a car.

But there is more to relocation than just writing a check to your employees for the moving expenses and giving them a date to report to work. Depending on their situation, there may be a "trailing spouse's" career and children to consider. I contact human resources directors for these trailing spouses to help them find work at their new location.

A new home, new schools, and a new neighborhood are just a few of the considerations of an employee who is being asked to move and uproot their lives.

As part of my business, I realized that I needed to probe deeper regarding the needs of the relocating employee and their family. In doing so, I was soon able to identify how I could benefit the employee and their employer. Then I began to work with these companies, offering them this specific assistance.

It quickly became a niche business within the real estate industry and one that has grown substantially over the years.

How was I filling this need for companies that had been there all the time? All I did was what most of the other agents were not doing. It started at the beginning of my relationship with people who were in the process of relocating.

As I mentioned, when I first meet people, I ask a lot of questions. Not just about the type of home they need, but also the type of activities and hobbies they enjoy doing. What are some of their favorite experiences? What is their typical routine like? How do they unwind? What does downtime look like in their home?

It means getting to know the individuals that are being relocated, beyond the number of bedrooms and bathrooms that they want. For employers, keeping an employee that has often been relocated depends on how happy they are in the new location and their ability to connect with their new community.

I have had people pick a home that fits them, but the location turned out to be less than ideal because it wasn't close to the amenities or schools they needed. In the end, they may have picked a great home but not a great location. When companies are choosing a real estate agent to assist in relocating their employees, I know, as the agent, that I have to be willing to do my homework and truly understand the needs of the individuals relocating.

In your business, are you doing your homework? Are you getting to know the needs of your business niche or are you just making blanket assumptions and hoping for the best? If you are not willing to do your homework, you might have identified an opportunity but be unable to take advantage of it and truly reap the benefits.

A great example of this is when a company is preparing to make a large capital investment. No company just buys the first big machine or the first computer program they see; it takes research. A large outlay of capital can have a positive or negative impact on the future of the company.

In my niche, I have an impact on the future of these companies as well. When employees have a relocation go badly, employers could find that their outlay of capital is wasted because the employee's productivity may go down or, worse yet, the employee may choose to leave the company altogether.

I determined that I can meet the needs of these companies and their employees by providing a service that adds value to the relocation process. I make the process smoother for the employees and in turn, the companies that hire them.

If you have identified a niche opportunity, can you provide the right services or products to answer the needs of an underserved market? Would it be better to partner with someone else who can bring additional skills to the table? To ignore your weaknesses in various areas could leave your business weak as well, and make it harder to grow over time.

Tap into the skills of your employees; use their expertise in various areas to grow your company. When I was in Virginia, my real estate business had multiple divisions because I used the individual strengths of my agents to capture diverse market share. And, I also understand that business is cyclical and that downturns are a part of business. Multiple divisions in my company helped to buffer the business as a result, even during the downtimes.

Finding the right home was only one aspect of the larger picture of my work, especially as it relates to my relocation services. I will now identify multiple areas where I provided unique insights that make me stand apart from others. This focus kept me at the top of this niche market with the largest employers in the area.

Some of the offerings that make me stand out include assisting a relocating family with concierge services and moving companies. I also acquaint my clients with their new surroundings by showing them where the shopping options, restaurants, and other amenities are located. Now, for me to truly stand out and meet their needs, I also request interior photos, furniture dimensions, and fabric samples of the buyer's current residence. I have flown on company jets to view cities, towns, homes, and even grocery stores in the areas where these transferees are leaving. I tailor my high level of service to these people's requirements, and this is how I create my own niche within the real estate industry.

Eventually, I relocated back to Hawaii and began working in the Oahu real estate market. As a real estate agent involved in relocating people, I want to make sure they are excited about their new home. Since I now live and work in Hawaii, it can seem easy to sell paradise, but there are aspects that individuals relocating to the islands need to consider.

One, the islands are beautiful, but they are a significant journey away from the Mainland U.S. For people that are leaving their support system, including close family and relatives, the inability to just hop in a car and drive to visit loved ones can be a difficult part of the transition to island life. The beautiful scenery and the amazing outdoor activities can inspire a family moving to the islands, but the reality of the distance from their inner social circle can be a unique challenge. As a real estate professional, I focus on finding out more about the family and then matching them with a neighborhood that will complement their interests. This makes it easier for them to transition and build a new social circle.

Two, if the buyers do not have children, then finding great schools may not be on their main list of needs. But, they might want to be closer to a variety of local restaurants or the beach. Experienced relocation real estate agents are going to focus on getting to know the family they are working with beyond the size of home they are looking for. Then, there are the natural questions about the type of property they prefer in terms of size, flow, and floorplan. All of the information gathered helps me to give the buyers a personalized experience, and many have chosen me repeatedly as a result.

In the same way, you need to be a resource for your clients, providing them knowledge that they may lack. As I educate my clients about island life, I am providing a unique touch that personalizes the experience for them. How can you personalize the experience for your clients? Can you meet the needs you have identified while also standing out in their memory because of the experience they had with you or your company?

When you build a niche business, you want to build excitement, but you also need to help your clients manage their expectations. For instance, your solution to fill a niche might not completely meet all of their needs, but you can at least get them closer to that point. Help them to focus on what they get from the experience, not what they do not. Let me explain using the real estate market in Hawaii.

In Hawaii, homes can be more expensive than on the Mainland. It is the reality of a smaller available inventory and the cost of building new homes. Construction costs are significantly higher in the islands, as a vast majority of supplies have to come over the ocean. For a relocating employee, there is the reality that their money may not buy as large a house here as they may have previously owned. This can be a significant adjustment.

At this point, I want to find out more about how my clients function as a group.

Since they may have to deal with less living space, it is important to make sure the space they do have is laid out well for them. In this way, I am managing their expectations and focusing them on what they will get from the adjustment to their living space, not what is being taken away from them.

Again, this goes back to getting to know the people. I ask a lot of questions and spend even more time listening. If you are not listening, you are not going to be able to do the best job possible for your clients. Remember, for them, the point of working with you and your company is to receive a positive experience overall, even if they do not get everything they want.

As I mentioned, I schedule a full day with my clients, not just hours. The reason is that while we are driving from house to house, I am learning about how they live. This information is not only helping me to find the right home for them but is also helping me to look for the right location as well. At times, it might be a property that needs some work but is in a location that fits their needs to a "T." The reason that I would still want to show them that property is because, while a house can be remodeled, the location cannot be changed.

There is also the impact of budgetary concerns when I am working with clients. They may have a house that needs to be sold back home, which means they have the concern of carrying two mortgages, or a rent payment and a mortgage. Relocation to areas where the cost of living might be significantly higher than what they have paid in the past can also be part of their sticker shock. It is part of the job of the relocation specialist to truly understand and address as many concerns as possible.

When I entered the relocation industry, there were not many businesses that offered what I did for companies. Many companies were amazed at the quality and quantity of services that I offered, which then led to more referrals. My business started to grow, and I kept my hand on the wheel. I created my own niche in the world of real estate.

What is your passion? What do you get excited about now? Take a moment to look at all the aspects in your life. Is there something that you enjoy doing that could be potentially valuable to someone else? This is key because what you enjoy is often where you can find and create a unique niche. It could be an off-shoot of an existing business or even build a new industry altogether. Many businesses that we rely on today as part of our normal everyday routine started out as a niche industry or business, created to fill a need that someone saw and monetized.

When there were no fax machines or internet, everything had to be hand-delivered and signed. Then, faxing and email arrived. Now, electronic signatures are the norm. But these ideas did not exist until someone came along and saw the potential to build a business around these products and services.

As an entrepreneur, you too have the same opportunity to build a business around a need that you discover. My real estate relocation service is about marrying both sides of the relocation coin, sellers who want to sell and buyers who want to own. Instead of a buyer or seller trying to coordinate everything by themselves, I provide the guidance from beginning to end.

As you find your niche, you may discover some areas of your business need to take a backseat to the line of growth. These less productive areas may need to be dropped from your services or products altogether because you simply cannot afford to take the time to work on that sideline. You just do not have enough clients wanting that service or product to make it financially worthwhile to remain in that area of business.

Still, while you are growing, remember that you have to manage the growth of your niche business. You do not want to grow so quickly that you outpace the demand of the market or end up putting yourself into debt. Your capital is something that needs to be used wisely to benefit your business. If you overleverage yourself, you run the risk of putting your business in jeopardy should the market take a turn for the worse.

How did I survive a time when companies were downsizing and not relocating as many employees?

I went back to some of the more traditional aspects of real estate, but I also kept my eye on the economy overall. Quality employees who provided real value to companies were still in high demand, so there was still business out there.

However, I needed to work even harder to achieve and maintain a high level of quality service that is exciting to clients. It was this excitement that kept the referrals coming, even as the market was driving thousands of real estate agents out of the business altogether.

During a downturn, the marketplace gets more competitive. The reason is that when there is a lot of business, everyone does well, even those businesses that do not always provide the greatest service. It's because there is a high demand that must be met.

But, when that demand disappears, the businesses that do not make quality their focus end up struggling to stay afloat or they go out of business. Why? Because all those companies that provide high-quality service are going after the same clients, and they are providing a better experience.

The mediocre companies eventually fall out because they cannot meet the clients' expectations, which have been enhanced by the competition in the marketplace.

When it is a buyer's market, companies need to up their game. This is especially true if you have built a niche business. However, even if your business is not being affected as profoundly by changes in the marketplace, you still need to be proactive in maintaining the growth of your bottom line.

Therefore, you need to be willing to do something new and continually be on the lookout for ways to provide something better for your clients. It means looking at change differently than you have in the past. It's more than just riding the waves of a shrinking market or an economic downturn; it's about thriving in the shifting seas of your industry.

As you start the next chapter, ask yourself: How do I see change? The impact of how you view change has a much larger impact on your business than you may realize.

Success Secret #4

See Change as an Opportunity

Throughout my years in the real estate business, I have been told plenty of things by individuals while in the car showing property which would surprise their employer. It could be anything from "I just want to relocate and then I'm leaving the company," to dissatisfaction with their employer in general, or with the fact that they had to relocate. As a rule, I approach these revelations as *what is said in the car, stays in the car.*

All of these various disclosures have shown me the numerous responses people can have to change in their lives. Some individuals see change as an obstacle or trial—something that must be endured. To them, change has a negative connotation, and they rarely see the positive aspects it can bring into their lives. The experience may remain a negative for years to come, just because of their perspective of the experience in the moment.

For me, change has always seemed to bring the next great adventure. Additionally, change has presented some unique and exciting financial opportunities. My income consistently increased as I started new businesses and explored the world outside of my comfort zone.

Running a restaurant, for example, is not easy. It requires hard work, consistency of your product, and quality service. But there is also the reality that a majority of restaurants fail. The economies of the restaurant industry mean that margins are small, and profits can quickly disappear in food costs and overhead.

So, how did I manage to build a successful business, one that was profitable within the first year? I created change by looking at the restaurant's possibilities versus the negative realities that could exist. I did not dwell on bad things that could happen but focused on what was possible. My mindset was not geared to failure but geared to success.

How do you view change? Are you seeing the possibilities or are you training your mind to focus only on the negative and what failure looks like? Doing so can often cause you to make choices that create the failure you focused on so intently. The same can also be true if you focus on the possibilities of what can and will happen if you embrace change.

There were a lot of possibilities in that restaurant. My partner and I built a solid customer base because we gave them quality food at reasonable prices with great service. We provided that every single time they sat down in our restaurant.

If you are seeking the opportunities in change, then you need to remember that change also requires effort from you. It is not as easy as deciding to start a business simply because you see the opportunity.

You also need to acknowledge the work and effort that will be involved. If you cannot give it your all, then you might be wasting valuable resources to chase a business that doesn't have your full attention; you will end up struggling or even failing as a result.

My income doubled consistently over time because I was always keeping my eye on the ball. I was hands-on and did not leave my business to be run by someone else. They were not going to give it the same time, energy, and attention that an owner would. At my restaurant, this meant always being aware of the costs involved in each product and training staff to make sure it was made the same way every time. I was available to my customers and staff, so I could quickly address their concerns and accept their valuable feedback.

Change was an aspect of my life that I embraced. Looking back, I feel it allowed me to have a richer life, with more varied experiences than I would have had staying in Detroit, Michigan.

If you are starting a new business, you may be creating a company that does something never seen before now. You will probably meet people who tell you that it is not possible and cannot be done. You may also meet people who said that they were going to do it but never did.

You need to decide if you want to create change based on the opportunity you see, that they do not. Or, do you want to follow the crowd and let change bypass you.

When I went into the restaurant business, I was not jumping in because of a financial need in my family or because I wanted to start a business that had never been done before. I simply saw an opportunity for our family. As an entrepreneur, you are also in the position of starting a business, but you might be pursuing it to fulfill a financial need or address a growing demand in the community. It is your vision and drive that often are so valuable.

Entrepreneurs are important, not just for the vision and innovation they possess, but for the overall economic impact they provide. That is right; you can have a large economic impact just by pursuing your business model. When you are successful, you can impact the overall standard of living for individuals and your larger community. The impact can be even greater if your business reaches a national or global level of clientele.

When Steve Jobs was trying to sell the earliest Apple® computers, he had a vision of the future and what society was going to look like. Today, we manifest his vision with our smartphones and tablets, etc. Apps are changing how we interact with others, and social media has driven change in our approach to relationships.

Not only that, but these businesses all create employment that did not exist before and market demand where there had been none. The tech industry has grown and become a staple in many cities, looking to create a welcoming home for these companies and the industry as a whole. Thirty years ago, many of these companies did not even exist. This growth undoubtedly affects additional industries, and so on into the future.

Think about your business or idea. What type of support functions might you need from businesses outside of your core industry? Your business will be helping them to grow as well. Entrepreneurs do not just bring jobs to their own industries; they bring jobs to a large number of other sectors—even some that might seem unlikely at first.

For instance, an entrepreneur choosing to open his business in a small town brings jobs as he or she hires for their business. Then, those employees increase demand on services and businesses around town. This means more people need to be hired to meet the need. An entrepreneur is like a wave in the ocean; you do not impact just one boat but potentially hundreds and thousands.

You are creating change for others by pursuing the opportunities change has presented for you. Do not just stop there. Nurture others around you to see change as an opportunity. You might be inspiring the next Bill Gates or Steve Jobs.

The next wave of your industry's growth could be someone that you nurtured to take a risk and embrace change. I also learned that change provides moments of growth on a personal level as well. Think back to my family for a moment.

The moving and constant upheaval that my children experienced growing up gave them a great deal of flexibility, both personally and professionally. They learned how to thrive, no matter what, in a variety of environments and cultures. It was also a cultural learning curve for me personally.

I was raised in a Midwest state, so my experience with race was different than many of those individuals born and raised in the southern United States. This was the 1950s and 1960s, so you have to remember that the country as a whole was undergoing some significant changes.

My husband was transferred to Kentucky. It was a trying move for us, as my oldest son was almost three, and I was almost nine months pregnant with my second child. Back then, no doctor wanted to take me as a patient because I was so close to delivering; no one wanted to be responsible if something went wrong.

I remember standing in a phone booth in the Kentucky heat, with a phone book, calling doctors, begging them to consider having me as a patient. Eventually, I found, a kindhearted doctor who delivered my second child.

After leaving the hospital, I asked a wonderful woman to come and assist me for two weeks with my baby and young son. She was referred to me by someone at my husband's work.

This lady was African-American, and that meant something different in the South at that time, as I was soon to learn. I wanted to show my appreciation for her help, so I invited her and her granddaughter to my son's third birthday party.

She declined my invitation. I asked her why; she explained that she and her granddaughter wouldn't be welcomed by the other guests.

Her explanation of the southern United States just floored me. I decided that I wasn't going to worry about what others thought, so I encouraged her to come anyway. She responded that she still wouldn't come but then told me that it was to protect her granddaughter.

Due to her race, the grandmother felt that the granddaughter might be treated differently and, as a family, they wanted to protect her from that as long as possible. Attending a birthday party for a young white boy could have brought the impact of those differences home to her much sooner than they wanted. It was a real eye-opener for me about how things were in the South at that time.

I learned something of cultural significance, but I also recognized that I couldn't necessarily reform a whole culture just because I saw things differently. My reach wasn't going to be as far as I might have liked, but I still had the opportunity to be an influence with the people in my circle, small as it was at that time. The little girl did end up attending the birthday party, and everyone had a great time.

As an entrepreneur, you are not only going to be challenged to thrive in the face of change but also in the face of cultural norms you might not agree with or even fully understand. Not every experience will be relaxed or enjoyable;

some will require you to step outside of your comfort zone. If you want to achieve success, you need to embrace these changes and challenges and not run from them.

As I have learned, you can also profoundly impact your community by embracing and creating change. It doesn't just have to be about economics. I draw people into a community through my real estate work, but also by how I treat them as individuals. My experience in Kentucky taught me that a community can be united or be divided, but it all depends on how you are willing to see others. Today, the communities I work in are enriched because of the people I help to assimilate there.

Perhaps your niche business will also provide some gift that develops or refines your community. Do not be quick to dismiss your impact. It could be much larger than just your bottom line. Not only do you need to be willing to embrace change and all that it brings, you can also be a leader who helps others embrace change as well. It all goes back to your mindset. Making a change in how you do things in your business can cause some discomfort. It is a risk, but one that you need to take in order to create the business that you want.

At the same time, when you make changes, you are going to be asking your employees to make changes as well. It can be risky because not everyone can adapt well to change. They may prefer the old way of doing things and want to keep that in practice, even if they are shown a way that is more productive, can be done faster, and can even reduce the number of steps needed overall.

Therefore, your employees will adapt best if they see you taking on changes with a positive attitude and embracing the new way of doing things. If you fall back into old patterns, they will too. Carve out the path, and show them how to reach for the goals that you have set for your business.

Do not complain about things you cannot change. Instead, replace complaints with requests for change from individuals, and take actions to achieve your goals.

Circumstances are always changing, so you need to adjust your reactions to meet those changes. Once you learn to respond quickly and decisively to the signals of change in the air, you put yourself in the driver's seat of your life and your business. Markets do have curves, and there are factors outside of your control that can impact your business. However, you are the one to decide how to respond to those factors and create the best outcome possible for your business and your employees.

Whether you see change as a good thing or a bad thing, you are right. This is because the experiences will shape themselves to meet your expectations. Make sure your expectations are focused on the success of the change, versus the negative. You will be amazed at how many blessings you will find after you change your mindset!

Change is now taking on a whole new light in your mind, is it not? But how can you effectively build a business based on your vision and the changes that you are experiencing in your own life? It often starts with two essential skills that every entrepreneur needs to be successful.

Are you ready to learn what they are and how they can impact your future? I'll give you a hint to what they both are: One requires your ears and your mouth; the other requires your muscles. Now that you have your guesses, read on to see if you are right!

Success Secret #5

Work Hard at Communicating with Your Clients

My life has been dominated by my work ethic. I remember from an early age that I was always looking for work and ways to contribute to the world around me. As a result, I was always busy working and going to school. No matter what I participated in, I was determined to be successful at it.

There is a certain mindset that you need to have to be successful in anything that you attempt. It is a determination that you will find a path to success, no matter how many obstacles may appear or detours you might take in your journey.

This mindset also includes a willingness to work hard, and you must communicate to others that you are willing to work hard as an example for them. There is a drive that you need to bring to any venture that you take on, no matter the industry. The entrepreneurs that are most successful are willing to get in there and get their hands dirty. They do the hard work needed to create a quality product or service and the systems necessary to deliver it consistently.

During my years as a restaurant owner, I was actively involved in all aspects of the restaurant. It meant diving into the financial aspects of the business but also understanding what was going on in the kitchen and the front of the house. Plus, I was still juggling the responsibilities of being a wife and mother to now three children.

Remember that working hard doesn't mean burning yourself out all of the time. I could have kept the restaurant open for dinner, but I would have been stretching myself way too thin, and no one would be getting my very best—not my family, and certainly not my restaurant.

I was accountable to the staff and those individuals who came to eat and relax at my restaurant. When you are working hard, remember to keep balance in your life. It can be easy to burn out if you do not take time for yourself.

Real estate also involves a lot of hard work and effort in terms of defining the needs of your clients and then scouring the available inventory for options that match that list. Part of my job is to avoid taking them on tours of homes that are far outside of their budget or would put them in a neighborhood that they would think does not match their lifestyle. It would be wasting their time and mine.

Sometimes people get so focused on what is not in a home that they miss the positives of the entire property and how it could truly fit their needs. I strive to help clients see the possibilities of the homes I am showing them. Good communication is the key to making this happen.

Hard work in real estate often means employing superior listening skills, the first step in good communication. What do I mean by that? When you think about connecting with your clients, you need to be able to understand them. You cannot discover what they need and want if you tune them out when they are talking, more focused on formulating your response before they are done expressing their thoughts and feelings.

This means giving your customers and clients your full attention; look them in the eye and acknowledging what they said by rephrasing it and repeating it back to them. You want them to feel comfortable with you, but that cannot happen if they feel you are dismissing them by not listening.

For me, superior listening skills involve more than just hearing what clients say; it is about looking at their body language and recognizing the things that they *are not saying*. Body language is a powerful medium and has a great impact on any discussion. After all, a client can be telling you that the house or meal is fine, but if their facial expression tells a different story, then you are going to want to dig deeper for more information.

Some business owners will take what individuals say at face value, without taking body language into consideration but this is a big mistake. If an individual is not truly happy with their experience with you, then they are not going to be repeat customers. They certainly are not going to recommend you to others. How you speak is also important. People have often told me that my calm voice has helped them feel good during the pressures of a real estate transaction.

Another essential piece to working hard is being a continuous communicator with your clients and your team. We have all had an experience where the process of getting something done was painful because there was a lack of direction and communication from the individual in charge, be it a work setting or even volunteering. The disorganization coming from a lack of continuous communication ultimately impacts your bottom line, no matter what type of business you have.

How can you be sure that you are communicating effectively? In many ways, it comes down to access to your audience, be it a client or an employee. If you are with them, what does their body language say? Does their facial expression suggest understanding, or do they appear confused and in need of more of an explanation? Not everyone is always going to hold up their hand and ask the questions that they need to ask.

As a leader, you need to anticipate this and address as many potential questions as you can think of in your presentation. It is also important to create an environment where questions are welcomed. Ask yourself: Am I approachable? Do my clients and employees feel comfortable around me?

This is essential. No matter how many questions or details you feel that you have addressed, there is always going to be something that you haven't thought of or may not have explained as clearly as you think. Part of great communication is getting feedback from your clients and team. They bring their experience, needs, and concerns. You want to tap into this to make your business better.

When it comes to clients, they need to be comfortable enough to tell you their expectations and if they are concerned that these expectations are not being met. Taking a client on a home tour can be a course in having your communication and listening skills tested to the maximum.

For instance, a client may tell you that they want an open floor plan with plenty of space for entertaining. You show them a space you feel completely fits the bill, but their face says otherwise. The potential issue is, now that they are in that big space, they realize how it echoes and, at the same time, how difficult it might be for the family to enjoy various activities without interrupting each other.

If you observe this, then you might want to suggest other properties without such an open floor plan. They expressed a want, but you must be able to discern their real needs by using your listening skills. You need to help make them feel comfortable enough to express their real thoughts about a property to you.

Approachability is a critical component of any business, and I can say it is absolutely necessary for a successful career in real estate. Your clients need to be able to share so many details about how they live. If they do not feel comfortable with you, then it will be impossible for you to give them the very best service.

Are your clients comfortable when they work with you? Do they feel as if they can share the positives and negatives of their experiences with your company? Or, do you find yourself cutting them off before they finish speaking, and making excuses for why things did not go as they should?

When you work with a client and are getting feedback, then you need to be prepared to hear the good, the bad, and the ugly. After the client has finished sharing their experience, be willing to address their concerns in a way that makes them feel that you have heard them.

Even if you cannot do everything that they need you to do, make sure you are not just making excuses. Offer viable alternatives to address their concerns. It might not be what they envisioned, but you may find that they are more excited about your optional suggestions in the end.

Since we do not always have the clearest vision regarding our actions and reactions, we might create tunnel vision that could allow us to miss signals that would tell us if change is needed. So, we must get feedback from others.

Ask for honest responses to the following questions. When asking your clients and employees, be prepared not to hear that everything is wonderful. But, take it as constructive feedback that can help you make the changes you need. Here are a few questions you can use to get the ball rolling:

- What am I doing that is working?
- What am I doing that is not working?
- What do I need to do more?
- What do I need to do less?
- What am I not doing that I should try and take a risk?

Also, I have learned that not every client knows what they want when they first sit down with you. This could be due to a lack of experience or not understanding the offerings available, or both. You may find yourself serving as an educator for your clients.

Do not be quick to shut down or assume that a client without a clear idea of their needs is not a valuable client who is worth your time and attention. By providing assistance and helping them focus on the direction they need to go, you could be gaining a repeat client and also plenty of referrals as they tell others about you in a positive light.

Your brand and reputation can grow by your willingness to work with a client who has not yet defined their needs completely. In the world of real estate, clients often have preconceived notions of what they want in a home. Once I get to know my clients, I find out what their lifestyle is really like. As a result, I can determine when their wish list is counterintuitive to the way they live daily and help them make choices.

As you listen to your clients, you will find that you become more aware of how they will be using your products or services. Perhaps you may find that they would be better served with another option. Be willing to say so, in a tactful way. It might not mean a sale for your business that time around, but it will increase your reputation as someone who is not just trying to sell for the sake of a sale. You will build credibility and word will get out in the community that your business is trustworthy. This will result in an increase in sales because clients are drawn to those who they trust.

That type of reputation is pure gold. Clients flock to businesses that have their best interests at heart, and when they know you are willing to communicate clearly and work hard for them. Make your clients feel they are getting your very best and they will respond in a way that grows your business and bank account!

Success Secret #6

Give 100% Every Time

Take a moment and think back to a time in your career when you were not as successful as you had hoped. What were the specifics surrounding that failure? Did you give everything you had to produce the best outcome for your clients or your employer? Or, can you honestly say that your heart wasn't in it?

In the various businesses where I have been privileged to work, one point has always stuck out to me. Those who give 100% end up with a 110% return and more. Giving your best always works in your favor. It might not seem so with every client, but over time, your reputation of giving that 100% effort will bring you an increase in business and grow your brand.

Take Starbucks® for instance. This is a company that serves coffee, tea, and various food products. They have not created new food ingredients, but what the company has done is create a positive, customer-centric model. Starbucks® has spawned a myriad of unique coffee and tea selections. They train their employees to give 100% with every single customer encounter. The employees do this well, and they have created an international following and a global brand. Starbucks® continues to build a massive customer base, creating an amazing experience with innovative, quality products.

Now, let's talk about what I do that gives my clients that 100% experience. First, I listen to them carefully. Again, truly listening is the biggest part of giving your client an experience they are sure to remember. When they see you actively responding to their requests, or doing your best to offer a comparable option, they feel the 100% effect.

If I were to listen to a client talk about their love of the city, then show them properties primarily within the suburbs, I definitely am not giving them 100%.

I might have to show them smaller properties in the city to meet budget considerations, but I still need to focus on the area where they want to live.

My personal preferences do not play a part in the process. Remember, when you are listening to and attempting to give your clients the best possible service, you need to be attentive. What you think is best will ultimately have no bearing on what they actually want. You can give them the benefit of your experience and skills yet; they ultimately will make their own decision.

Sales have always been a huge part of my life. I have always been marketing myself, or one of my businesses, and making proposals to draw individuals into trying out my business. I also must cater to my long-time and repeat clients; if they do not have that same 100% experience every time, they will not be a client for long.

How can you achieve that 100% experience with every interaction? It also starts by being 100% accountable to yourself and your clients. If you are quick to make excuses or put the blame on an employee or supplier, your clients will quickly find another business to work with. They do not want excuses; they want results!

No matter which business I was running at the time, the buck stopped with me.

I am the leader and set the tone for what occurs in my business, and the experience my clients receive. If you want to be successful, then you need to take 100% responsibility for all aspects of your business.

You have the power to get it right, to make changes, and to produce an amazing experience for your clients every single time. If you do not get the results that you want, then you need to ask yourself why. It means that you become the detective in your own business, ferreting out the reasons why things are not going as you planned. Here are just a few potential questions to ask yourself:

- What was I thinking?
- What did I say or not say?
- What did I do or not do to create that result?
- What do I need to do differently to get the result I want next time?

These questions are geared to changing your responses to circumstances, therefore allowing you to create the outcomes you want. It is how you think about the circumstances and adjust for them that defines your outcome. You can choose your attitude and behavior, which can greatly impact your business and its level of success.

We have control over our thoughts, what we visualize, and what actions we choose to take. There is nothing else that we can control, and how you choose to use these three things can alter what you produce and experience. If your business is not as successful as you would like, then you need to look at how you are acting and reacting. What type of thoughts are you having? What are you visualizing? Are you focusing on the negative or looking for the positive?

You may also have habits that are impeding your ability to be successful. I have been in real estate for some time and have found that clients do not like to be rushed. They are making a big financial decision; so, of course, they want to make sure they are truly committed to the home that they have chosen. Do your clients need more time to think or ask questions, but you have limited that time in order to get more clients in and out of the door? It might mean changing how you schedule clients to achieve a better connection and better results.

It is not always easy to implement this idea of being 100% responsible for how your business performs. It requires you to be aware of what is going on, both internally in your business and externally in the marketplace and industry.

Look at the results you are producing. Results do not lie, and they can be a point of reference regarding areas that need your attention. Once you decide the results are not to your liking, then trace back to the actions or methods you used to produce them and, start making changes. Your business will be successful if you have the right mindset to make it that way.

Do not believe, just because your industry is going through a downturn that you cannot thrive. If you think positively, then you will achieve the results that meet your expectations. Taking responsibility for your business is not always easy. There is a tendency to want to blame someone else or make external factors the culprit. When you give 100%, in terms of responsibility and how you treat others, then you will reap that 110% plus return business model and achieve your goals.

Now, part of taking 100% responsibility involves taking risks. You are not always going to be comfortable as you acknowledge the part that you have played in getting your business to where it is today. For those who are risk-averse, this part can be difficult to do. After all, you have to admit that in some ways it can be easier to put the blame on others or complain than be the catalyst to change your results. But, if you are willing to change your attitude, your thoughts, and your actions, you can create an amazing new future for your business.

You can meet your goals by taking full responsibility for your business and your results. Your clients and employees will see that you are fully invested in your business, and that will get them excited to be involved. They will receive a 100% experience because that is what you create. The choice is, and always has been, up to you!

Now, let's talk about what is involved when you choose to take a risk and how it can impact your goals and the future of your business.

Success Secret #7

Be Willing to Take a Risk

Throughout my career, I was presented with plenty of chances to play it safe and take the easy road. We are all presented with those moments, and it can be tempting to play it safe. But as a true entrepreneur, I can say that those easy paths with limited risk was not for me. I would say that to be a successful entrepreneur you need to be willing to accept risk and take it on, even if the path to your goals is difficult as a result.

The rewards often outweigh the risks, particularly in terms of the experience you gain. Imagine all those moments in your life when you fell. After you got back up, you could look back and see the knowledge and wisdom you gained. In the world of entrepreneurship, risk can involve a fall now and again. But these falls are the chance for you to grow, both personally and professionally.

When we first opened the restaurant, my partner and I did not know how to run this type of business. We did not know about cooking for the public; our experience was limited to fixing the right size meal for our families. It meant learning how to make certain recipes in larger quantities and to adjust the recipes for single servings in other cases. I should note here that we also ran a catering business out of the restaurant as well. There was also the reality of handling a payroll and managing a variety of expenses, in addition to caring for our customers in a way that made them want to come back to our restaurant. There was definitely a lot of risk in that business.

But, we weighed that risk and decided to go for it anyway. I can promise you that I never regretted taking that risk. The restaurant was not only successful but when it was time to relocate yet again, I was able to sell it for a nice profit. The restaurant, although with different owners, is still open today. It has remained a positive part of the community, with a different menu.

You may find that as you create and grow your business, it can outgrow you.

In these instances, it might require a new leader to continue on the path, which means that you need to step out of the way. Take pride in what you have accomplished, but do not let your pride limit the potential of what you have started. Sometimes the risk you take is the one where you walk away from your creation.

At this point, I also have to point out that not every business model or plan is realistic. Not every business will be a success. You may find that you have created one of those. Making the decision to shut it down is also a risk, but you might see this as your best option.

However, I can tell you from experience that when one door shuts, another one always seems to open up for me. You need to be aware of what is going on around you to find that next opening or opportunity.

Networking is one of the most important ways to keep your ear to the ground for new opportunities. As you build your network, you can find a business looking for a partner to bring in additional capital. You may also find a need that is going unfilled, which could be a potential business opportunity. More about networking later.

When I first entered real estate, I was focused on learning the business and providing the best service possible to my clients. Of course, I was listening to my clients and, over time, I saw a niche that was not being met for corporate clients. As companies attempted to relocate employees, there were issues with getting the old homes sold and new homes found.

It became a logistical issue that was overwhelming the employees who needed to move and get their family settled, often on a tight timeline. The question was how the company could get their employee relocated and assist with the logistics? At first, I was just helping them find rentals, but over time, it grew into something more. It was a risk for me to start this new relocation business, but I did it anyway.

I would help employees find their new home while consulting with them about getting their old house ready for sale. Now, I was fulfilling a need, but also creating a business within a market that was full of real estate agents.

In hindsight, it was risky for me not to pursue this specialized area of real estate.

My work helps to relieve the transferees' stress because I truly got to know what they need in their new home and neighborhood. It is important to remember that these transferees were also taking a risk on a new job or assignment. Risk is a necessary part of life.

When you are taking a risk, and seizing a new opportunity to build a service that caters to a specific market niche, it is important to find unique aspects of your service that makes you stand out from the crowd. I do this by offering services that make my clients feel comfortable working with me. For example, I use my experience in selling homes to provide advice on staging and presenting the houses properly. I provide so much more in terms of quality service that individuals and companies come to me.

My staging expertise includes everything from initial interior and exterior preparation to final staging. I work with the furnishings that my clients have and am also able to use my contacts to rent additional pieces of furniture and art if needed, which will show their property in the best light. Selecting the right photographer for the home is also of great importance. For clients who are worried about finding a new home, packing, and selling their old house, this kind of advice is critical for them to move forward in a timely manner.

When you look back over your career, are there areas of expertise you possess that could be turned into a business opportunity? Could you be providing a service that fills an underserved or unmet need in your industry or marketplace? Sometimes the question is not finding another position in a company to advance your career, but growing a business of your own by tapping your expertise.

Part of risk-taking is also recognizing when an industry might no longer be a good fit for you and, instead, taking your skills and branching out into a new area. While certain skills are naturally industry-specific, there are many skills that can be adapted to fit into a new market or niche outside of your current industry. Do not be afraid to take a risk and explore these types of changes. Doing so could open a whole new world in terms of your career and where you are headed.

When I look around in my industry, I find that the most successful individuals are the ones who are willing to go out on a limb, take a risk, and try something outside of their comfort zone.

Not every risk meets with success, but all risks allow you to learn something about yourself and the direction in which you want to take your career. Working is meant to be a way to earn a living, but it is important that you also enjoy the work that you do.

What do you enjoy doing? Have you ever thought about how you could monetize that activity? Do not assume that just because it is a hobby that there is little income to be made or limited success that can be achieved.

There are many products and services out there that started in someone's kitchen or garage and became success stories. They decided to monetize it and take the risk of going to the marketplace. These individuals took a step forward, even though they were not sure of the outcome. Yet, they could see the product being successful and they worked toward that vision.

Growing a new business includes finding, and perhaps even defining a market for your products or services. This could mean that you have to not only create a sales dialogue, you might have to educate your clients as well.

My business, for example, has more complexity than most people realize. In real estate, I spend almost as much time educating my clients about what is involved in buying or selling a house as I do showing properties and working on paperwork. For many, this paperwork might as well be in code. There are also inspections, property records to review, surveys, often financing details, and so much more. However, I do not give tax or legal advice even though our industry uses documents that can become legally binding.

My real estate expertise is essential in teaching my clients and finding them a home, in their budget, that meets all of their needs, or to sell their property.

If my clients thought they could do the job as well themselves, they wouldn't have hired me to be their real estate expert.

When you look at your own expertise, remember that it has value for someone, not just inside your industry but outside of it as well. This is because people need to tap into your knowledge without going through all the time and effort to learn it themselves. Capitalize on that need, and you can build a business that will grow by billing yourself as a qualified expert.

When I started the restaurant, I remember knowing that I was taking a risk. If the restaurant had not been successful, that would have been a blow to my reputation, but it also would have meant that I had spent time and energy in an unproductive way.

While we learn something from every failure or risk that we take, it is also important to calculate the costs of any venture before we begin. It might be worth the loss of family time temporarily in the beginning, but what are the long-term needs of the business going to be? Resources and capital are not just defined by money. They also include your time and energy which are valuable resources as well.

When you are deciding to take a risk, it is important to factor in all the costs.

My restaurant could have grown to include a dinner hour, which would have made us even more money, but the cost of time away from my family would have negatively impacted my life and that of my family. The answer was not to grow the restaurant in that direction. It might have meant an increase in profits, but the risk to my family's stability was not worth it.

Risks are necessary, and weighing the costs is reasonable. Remember that the risk should open an opportunity for you to meet your end goal, whatever that may be. Think of the end goal you have in mind, and everything else will makes sense as you continue to make decisions about your business. This is how your mind works. You might not be looking to create a business, but perhaps you are looking for a passive income stream. Investing could provide that, but there are still risks to consider and weigh.

Without risks, there are no rewards. If you always play it safe because there is a chance you might fail or lose, then you will find yourself stuck in your career and your life. If your life is reaching a crossroads, do not see that as a chance to do what you have always done. Take it for the opportunity that it is—to attempt something new.

All my relocations throughout my life gave me a chance to try my hand at living in a variety of places and exposed me to an assortment of individuals and industries.

I embraced the change in my life and, as a result, my life was enriched. When you are willing to embrace change in your life and take those risks, you will be amazed at how quickly your life will be enhanced and full of possibilities.

Risk means taking a chance without having a clearly defined outcome. Uncertainty is part of our daily lives, even if we do not always recognize it. But, if you do not expose yourself to uncertainty, you will not build the skills necessary to cope with life's challenges. Risk gives you the skills to problem solve, regulate stress and emotion, and take initiative in all areas of your life. Risk can improve your skills and help you work better with others in your life and career. Risk inspires you to grow.

Challenges are often risks wrapped in circumstances that you are presented with on a daily basis. As individuals, you never stop learning and growing unless you choose to. That means you are not destined to continue to live a certain way or make certain decisions. Instead, you can take these challenges and use them as opportunities to be successful in reaching your long-term goals.

Part of risk is recognizing that you have big ambitions for your life and that the risk of change can be transformational versus incremental. Transformational changes require you to think big, take big risks, and then learn to deal with them. There are definitely benefits, and remember that big risks can be calculated, and not just be a leap of faith.

Here are just a few of the potential benefits of taking risks:

- Learning new skills
- Breaking through self-imposed limits
- Becoming more creative
- Clearly defining what you want
- Uncovering unforeseen opportunities
- Growing your self-confidence
- Learning to trust yourself more
- Achieving your dreams and goals

Taking risks is not a personality trait; it is a decision-making process that allows you to embrace uncertainty. It means calculating the costs before you jump, but with the fundamental understanding that you cannot predict every outcome, every time. However, you have control over how you react to the outcomes and circumstances that present themselves.

Taking charge of your own thoughts, responses, and attitude is key to taking risks. Embrace what happens when you jump in, versus waiting on the sidelines. Once you taste success, you will continue to want to take risks to achieve even greater goals than you might have previously imagined.

Part of risk-taking is embracing the wonders of change. When you do so, you are not falling behind in your chosen industry, but you can actually set the pace. It is important to remember not to focus only on what could go wrong, but what could go right as well.

Without risk, you might look back on your life and find that the direction you have taken meant missing out on plenty of adventures, both personally and professionally.

Life is full of risky decisions, but if you embrace them, you can take your life in some surprising and rewarding directions!

Success Secret #8

Always Look for Ways to Grow – Mentors, Networking & Coaches

Throughout my career, I have been an employee and a business owner. I have found a niche in the restaurant industry and established myself as an expert in the field of real estate. No matter what I did, however, I was always looking for growth opportunities.

In the restaurant, I did not just want to serve food. I wanted to create a business that could expand. Not only did we look at expanding in terms of locations, we were also creating our own line of food products, based on recipes used in the restaurant. I planned to create my own line of dressings and products before it was as commonplace as it is today.

Why was I willing to take that risk? I saw it as a chance to grow. As you build your business or career, you are going to take risks. The reality is that risks, as we have already discussed, are key to your growth path. This is because risk can open the door to opportunities, and that is where growth happens.

However, what if the roadblock to your growth is not available opportunities but understanding how best to leverage them? At this point, mentors are essential to your growth and success. When you find a mentor in your field or industry, you are going to be able to tap into their experience and wisdom.

Part of your success is found by seeking out guidance and advice from experts in their fields. Why not tap that vein of wisdom, versus using trial and error, which can end up costing you more than just a little time and effort?

Mentors can often help you to overcome any *possibility blindness* that you might have. This is because they act not only as a role model but also provide a certain level of expectation as they speak with you. They want to see you succeed.

As a business owner, you might not see potential in an opportunity, simply because your focus is somewhere else. A mentor, however, does not have that same focus, and they can provide you with a different, but critically important, perspective on your situation.

Mentors can also be a source of referrals, therefore providing another avenue of growth for you and your business or career. After all, they have more connections in your industry, allowing you to network with others to find doors of opportunity. Essentially, the mentor is there to show you where those doors are and even give you suggestions on how to open them. But, you have to be the one actually to open the doors of opportunity and step through them.

Another crucial part of having a mentor is that they may not only validate the path you are on, they can also assist you in determining the next steps to take. Are you having trouble determining what the next step for your business might be? Try talking it over with your mentor. It doesn't need to be a long conversation, but again, you are tapping their unique perspective on your situation.

You might be excited about getting a mentor. Unfortunately, they are not in a special aisle at your local grocery store. It will take effort on your part to find a mentor who is right for you.

The question is: How do you find a mentor? One of the easiest ways is to simply start looking for those who have been successful in your specific industry. Trade magazines, trade associations, trade shows, and the internet are all great places to start doing your research. Also, do not be afraid to call fellow entrepreneurs to ask who they would recommend.

The best mentors are those who have the well-rounded experience you need to achieve your goals. They are in a position to offer you great advice on how to improve your skill set. However, you cannot just start the conversation in a blind fashion. It is critical to have a list of specific points you would like to ask them about, including the type of help that you seek.

Also, you need to recognize that your mentor of choice is busy themselves. Make sure that you are respectful of their time, as you would expect someone to be of yours.

Then you need to be persistent. After all, once you have a list of potential mentors, you may find that not all of them are interested in mentoring you. When you make the request and receive a *yes*, do not squander the opportunity. Be available and open to what they have to say.

At the same time, you need to be willing to return the favor with your mentor. If you hear about an opportunity that might interest them, let them know about it. As you grow, eventually you might be able to mentor someone else. Always be willing to pass on your experience and the wisdom you have gained. Doing so can benefit your industry. It can also give you the next great employee for your own business!

I have been in real estate for many years, and one of the main ways I was able to make connections and grow in my industry was through networking. As you network, remember that it is not something you do at the beginning of your career and stop once you reach a certain level of success.

If you want to keep leveling up, it is important to build relationships. No matter what industry you are in, you need to nurture your relationships with your employees, colleagues, clients, and advisors.

A relationship forms when individuals spend time interacting with each other. Yet, I am sure that you have had experiences where the connection wasn't truly authentic and genuine. Did you want to do business with them again? Not likely.

Statistics have shown that people are most likely to do business with people who they know, like, and trust. If you build that type of relationship with clients, you will end up with repeat clients, which means your sales will grow consistently.

Here are just a few of the main benefits of networking and building up relationships with those around you:

- Generating Referrals – In real estate, referrals are key to growing your business. Individuals who are selling their home are quick to call friends and ask them who they used to sell their home and question them about their experience with that agent. When you create a positive experience for a client, it is one of the best ways to market yourself and your business.

  Over time, you can turn referrals into clients, which can lead to more recommendations. These referrals can end up being the higher quality leads that assist your business to grow.

- Expanding Opportunities – Networking with other business owners is also a great way to create joint ventures, share client leads, create partnerships, and so much more. If you are looking to invest in another business, then they might have a lead on a potential venture. You might also be able to satisfy the needs of a client who requires different skills than you have in your business. Therefore, you get a satisfied client, and both businesses have an increase in sales.

- Creating Connections – How many times have you heard the expression, "It's not what you know, it's who you know." This has never been truer than it is today due to social media. As you build your network, you are also tapping into the networks of other individuals. Building these relationships can help you to connect with influential people who might not have otherwise been available.

- Receiving Useful Advice – As you network with other business owners, you can take advantage of the opportunities to tap the advice and expertise of those individuals. Doing so will help you to be more aware of potential opportunities as they arise.

The reality of networking is that it is not the same as direct selling. It is about creating and building a network of individuals who know and trust you, therefore making them willing to do business with you, either now or in the future.

In order to create those relationships, you need to understand the steps involved. First, it is about being visible to someone you want to get to know. You can do this through your attendance at various industry events, through your advertising and public relations efforts, and volunteering.

Eventually, you start forming links in your relationship through different forms of contact. It could be quick phone calls regarding your services or another question about your business. Time allows the relationship to grow; that is how you create the recognition and awareness needed to take the relationship to the next level.

Do you know someone who you wouldn't do business with? Why is that? You would probably answer that you heard something about how they do business, or that you had a personal experience with them, which makes them less credible in your eyes. Credibility is a critical part of building your network. You want people to know that they can count on you and that you will follow through.

Some of the best ways to build your credibility are some of the simplest: Keep your appointments; always verify your facts; keep your promises; and deliver the best services possible. Results speak to your clients better than anything you could ever say to them. If you fail to live up to the expectations of your client or a member of your network, simply by not following through, then you can destroy the relationship.

Now, remember that networking is about creating relationships, but they will not last long if they are not mutually beneficial to each party. You have to be willing to give and take, not just take.

With a mutual payoff, you are likely to see that relationship grow and flourish, which means more business for you and more available resources that both of you can tap.

The best part of networking is that it doesn't have to be limited to just trade events or gatherings specifically geared to networking. Instead, those opportunities can literally be found anywhere.

I could start conversations about housing while standing in line waiting to pay for my lunch or picking up my dry cleaning. It is amazing how many people want to pick your brain once they realize you are a real estate agent. They ask questions about the current market, which neighborhoods are the best, and the list goes on and on.

Do you have the opportunity to talk about what you do in casual settings? You might be surprised at how you can end up with potential leads just from striking up a conversation while standing in line.

None of these connections or potential leads can go anywhere, however, without taking the time to follow up with them. Every follow-up might not mean that you receive something, but the relationship continues to grow with each connection and reconnection. The point is that follow-up is often what ends up getting results, not just making the initial connection. Following up is also important even after the initial sale has occurred.

This is because those reconnections build the relationship and can contribute to a higher level of trust and credibility over the long-term.

Finally, I want to point out that sharing your goals and dreams with others can end up helping you make the connections you need to achieve them. Time after time, talking with others in my industry, and also outside it, was what helped me to find the resources I needed to succeed. I wasn't necessarily focused on networking, but those casual conversations often lead to bigger things.

My real estate business grew on the East Coast because of the connections I made with various members of the industry who wanted to have me take business off their hands because it wasn't part of their specialty. Plus, I was able to make connections with larger companies that were looking to relocate their headquarters to our area. These connections allowed me to grow my business.

What amazes me is how often, by networking, you can find individuals who are simply too busy to take on additional lines of business. You could end up being their helping hand, but you will not know it if you are not willing to get out there and make connections.

Throughout this chapter, I have focused on the importance of growth through networking and mentors. Both options can help you to grow individually but also give your business a chance to grow as well.

One other way to grow, however, is by means of a personal coach. Using a personal coach, you can clarify your goals and have someone help you to follow the path that you have set to reach them. A coach can assist you in changing behaviors and habits that might be setting you back or keeping you from reaching your goals.

Coaches are effective because they work with you specifically to reach your goals and you are paying them to do it. Coaches are there to help you determine the actions needed to reach these goals and hold you accountable. Coaches also assist you in determining if an opportunity will be a stepping stone to reaching those goals or not; a coach can redirect you when you get side-tracked from your main priorities.

Many who have tried a personal coach find it to be a rewarding experience. The true value of a coach lies in their ability to encourage you, give you necessary insight and hold you to your word. Coaches can motivate you when the going gets tough, and they can be found based on a specific area of expertise or a specific industry.

Finding a coach can be as simple as doing an internet search. For the best results, consider looking within your own industry. Coaching has become a big business, and one that requires you to be specific about what you want to achieve and get out of the experience.

Ultimately, you need to be the catalyst to create growth in your business. But with these individuals in your corner, you can achieve your goals faster and with results that exceed your expectations. I know that many of the successes I had were not just due to my own abilities but because I was willing to be open to learning from others and applying what I learned.

It wasn't always easy because there were times when I would take on tasks that did not initially make me any money. But, by sticking with it and building my network, I eventually was able to accelerate my earnings and build a thriving business.

Today, I work in real estate assisting people to make the move to or sell in Hawaii. I help people own, sell and invest in homes, condominiums, and land.

My services also include using my network of REALTORS® around the United States and the world to find homes or sell property for people like you.

It is not always easy to keep networking and following up with people.

Finding mentors and coaches can be hard work, and you are not always going to be successful on your first try. However, if you are always looking for ways to grow, you can create that growth, personally and professionally!

Service After the Sale

It is important to remember that the sale doesn't end when the paperwork is signed and the transaction is completed, or when the service has been provided.

In order to truly grow a business, you need repeat clients. The reality of any business is that it is less expensive to keep a client than it is to obtain a new one.

But, keeping a client is more than just providing goods and services; it is about building a relationship through service after the sale.

What do I mean by service after the sale? It means making yourself available to your clients. You need to help them with any questions and provide personal touches that makes you and your company stand out from the crowd.

For me, my clients know that they can call me for information about the home, service professionals, or just about anything, even after I have helped them make their purchase or sale. I am thrilled when past clients call me to help them sell their properties too. When working with your clients, you want to take the worry out of the process for them. This builds trust, which is critical to building and maintaining a long-term relationship with your clients.

One of the best ways to build trust in a relationship is to start a conversation. It is not always about going in with your strongest sales presentation, but discovering whether or not you have the right solution for your clients. If you do, then your presentation of that solution, along with quality service, will get you that first sale and many more. You have to set a standard of service that your clients will come to expect every time.

When you cannot deliver that standard, you need to be honest and tell your clients. Give them this information so they can see you are trustworthy. Answer questions honestly and focus on what you can do for the client versus what you cannot.

Opening conversations involves focusing on specific challenges, which gives your clients the opportunity to come to you in the future, bringing you into their buying or selling process. If trust cannot be established, however, honest communication is not possible, and that means the relationship is unlikely to grow.

Over the years, I have found that pushing clients for repeat business has rarely brought me the sales I would like. However, clients know that they can contact me to answer their questions without me always pressing them for a sale. This means that I can probably obtain their business at a later date if they are not ready to own or sell now. Also, they have a positive experience with me that can result in them referring clients to me.

Are your clients seeing you as an aggressive salesperson and they dread taking your calls? Do they call you? Your clients or customers should see you as a source of knowledge and solutions to surmount their obstacles and fix their problems.

As I mentioned, when I first entered the real estate sales field, I worked with Tom Hopkins as a marketing director. Tom's personable nature made people want to do business with him. Tom created a warm and friendly atmosphere where people did not feel pushed into making a decision. One of the points that kept coming back to me was that he did not forget his clients after making a sale. Tom kept in touch with them, and this encouraged his clients to come back to him for additional help. The result was that his sales kept going up consistently. It was his example that helped fuel my own real estate sales.

As you can see, mentors and coaches are key to teaching you what you need to know to continue to grow and build your relationships with clients. Building a relationship with a client is not just for your benefit; it helps your clients as well. There are so many ways to serve your clients by helping them get the most out of your products or services.

As part of your sales process, make sure that you create natural touch points. Check in with the client after the sale to make sure they are continuing to have a positive experience with your company, and they will promote you and your brand. There was a reason your clients came to you, and the follow-up services that you offer can be the way to add value and really *wow* them.

One way to do so is through pairings of products and services. Think about when you make a purchase of a new cell phone. One of the quickest and easiest things to do is to provide accessories that the buyer can purchase at the same time. Not only is the sale larger, but the client's experience is being enriched, making it likely that they will come back to your company again for their next cell phone.

How do you support your product or service? Do you provide a way for clients to contact you with questions or assistance with installations? In real estate, there is a mountain of paperwork to track for the mortgage, closing, title work, and more. By taking the time to walk my clients through the process and being a resource for them, I am branding myself as a real estate professional who can provide them with support and experience, not just house tours.

Also, when you are looking for opportunities to help your clients, look for products and services that will give them a better experience. You do not want just to sell them something that they may not be happy with later. The reason is, if you are not sensitive to your clients' concerns, they are unlikely to return and, even worse, they are less likely to refer you to others.

If your business has new offerings on a regular basis, make sure that you keep your current and former clients in mind. Make them the first to know about your latest offerings. Also, as part of your relationship, keep up with their needs and any changes they might be experiencing in their lives or businesses. You might find that a new product or service coming out could be the answer to their needs.

In real estate, clients can have changes in work or family that mean they must relocate. They could also be looking for properties to invest in and use to create a passive income source. By keeping these clients' needs in mind, when I see a property come onto the market that might fill those needs, I give them a call.

That extra service keeps our relationship growing, and they are more likely to keep coming back to me in the future.

Client loyalty programs are another great way to keep clients engaged with your brand or company. The reason is that you are rewarding them for doing repeat business with you. If you do not have one, then consider brainstorming with your sales team to come up with one. You will be amazed at how effective a client loyalty program can be at drawing your clients back to your business.

Now, let's talk about referrals. I have mentioned how important they are to the growth of your business throughout this book. Here are just a few ways to get referrals and why they are so important to taking your business to the next level. However, keep in mind that an industry, such as real estate, might have limits on what you can legally offer your clients for referrals.

Effective referral programs are important to helping your clients develop routines that include your business. Think about your local coffee shop. Their loyalty program might be a free beverage after the purchase of five. This means that the customer might not have stopped by the coffee shop on the weekend, but they will because of the free drink. They are unlikely only to get their free drink, and more often than not, are going to make an additional purchase of food or other extras. The end result is that the additional sales often more than make up for the free product.

That loyalty program also can become a talking point for referrals because clients will talk about their free products. These rewards are often a cost-effective option to bring clients back, as well as bring new ones in the door. The rewards shouldn't be too hard to achieve, making it more likely that your clients will follow through with your reward plan.

Still, I have a few cautions about referrals. No one likes to be pushed to provide a referral. So, when you are asking for a referral, focus on the benefits of your products and services, not just the referral itself. Talk up the benefits that you would offer a potential referral, and your client will be more willing to give you those new potential leads.

Offer clear and simple directions for your customer or client to direct referrals to your business and receive their reward. If the referral program is too complicated, then they are unlikely to use it, and you will be losing potential business.

It can look easy to copy another business and try to reproduce their referral or reward program. The problem is that you might be copying a system that is not really a good fit for your business. Be creative and find the right reward system for your business and your clients.

The best way to create your referral and reward program is to think about what you offer and the needs of your clients, as well as your company's sales strategy. When you factor these all together, you will likely find the perfect fit for your business.

The reason referrals are so important is because they are one of the best ways to grow your business. If you have provided quality service to your clients, these people are likely to tell others. Once they do, those clients are providing a level of trust and a reference that can help other people want to come to your company first. Most clients love to feel that they are receiving personalized care and attention. When you provide that, their referrals will expect it too. So, you need to make sure that your clients always feel as if they are receiving top-notch service, and they will become a sales force for your business.

Use social media to your advantage. Invite your current clients to follow you through various social media channels and allow them to share your posts and comments. Doing so will allow word of your business to spread in an organic and viral way through their friends' lists. Do not be quick to dismiss these shares. Someone you would never guess might just contact you because of a post they saw in their news feed.

In real estate, people often talk about the houses they are interested in and share listings of houses they like. Consider doing the same. If you have a product or service you want to highlight, share it with your clients via social media. Talk about the benefits of the product or service, but do not make it a pushy sales ad. Your current clients could then use that post to share their own experiences with your company. The possibilities are endless.

Another point to keep in mind is the need to answer your clients promptly, and I know this sounds like a no-brainer. If you are not getting back with them right away, including after the sale, they are mentally storing this opinion of you. It may factor into whether or not they will do business with you again or tell others about your business. If you cannot help them when they call, be sure to help them find a solution with someone who can. Being generous with your time and attention shows your clients that you really care, and they are more than just a number.

Finally, as part of building your relationship, make sure you address complaints quickly and courteously. Even if you cannot completely fix the problem, handling the complaint well can turn a dissatisfied client into one that is a loyal advocate for your brand. Still, in order to effectively handle complaints, you need to have a clear policy in place that allows your staff to give the best possible service to your clients. Consider going to the clients' workplaces, if necessary, to solve the issue, versus just trying to deal with it over the phone or via the internet.

Always encourage your clients to bring their problems or concerns directly to you. Thank them for giving you feedback to help you address the problem and fix it. Consider rewarding them for bringing the issue to your attention. This will make them feel as if they are a valuable part of your business.

Your relationship building skills need to make your clients feel like part of your business, similar to an extended family. By offering them enhanced services, even after they have completed their purchase or sale, your clients will be more likely to come back and do business with you again. They will often bring others with them.

As you can see, follow-up is always going to be central to building and growing your business. Service after the sale never stops if you want to Double Your Income—you need always to be focusing on relationship building, both with your clients and the referrals that they bring to you.

Take Action to Create Your Amazing Career

Throughout this book, I have shared the lessons I have learned in my professional and personal life. The thing that I want you to remember is that none of those lessons would have been possible if I had not been open to taking action and growing my own abilities, knowledge, and experience.

When you look at your own career, it is important to find those areas that you can improve on and truly grow. It is about more than being a good communicator or leading effectively. You need to be able to see the opportunities that no one else notices, and then take advantage of them.

I was frequently relocating, due to my former husband's job opportunities. I did not have the luxury of growing my career in a traditional path of promotions and working consistently within one specific industry. I had to forge my path through business ownership. Due to my hard work and willingness to take risks, I was able to grow not one, but two different successful businesses. At the same time, I had to determine what my priorities were.

When I was opening the restaurant, I had to work with my partner to define how much we were willing to put into it and how we were going to balance the responsibilities of our families with the needs of our business. This meant that we opted out of keeping the business open later and adding to our overhead. But our focus on quality never wavered. The result was a viable business that remained profitable long after I sold it.

I want you to take the time to assess your career and business. Are you giving your clients the best in terms of quality? Are you really listening and communicating well, so that they feel their needs are being met? Have you determined your priorities, so that your business doesn't overwhelm your life?

Striking all the right balances in our lives can be challenging, but at the same time, without taking risks, we cannot truly tap into all of our potential.

I also believe that giving 100% in terms of effort for your business will result in happy clients and a successful brand. Growth happens when clients see your business as the best option to meet their needs. Your reputation will also draw clients to you through repeat clients and referrals. If you do not make your business a priority during the time set aside for it, then you will not reap the benefits or see the growth that you have envisioned.

As we have discussed, the realities of being a business owner means you are naturally taking a risk. At times, the circumstances can mean accepting a loss and closing a business, or even selling a business to someone who can make it viable because of their unique experience. Do not be afraid to restart if necessary.

Part of the beauty of relocating so many times is that I learned to embrace the joys and blessings of change. As an entrepreneur, it is important that you never get stuck in doing things a certain way and leave yourself in a position of falling behind in your industry. Fear of change will eventually put you behind the competition, instead of leading the pack.

Remember that industries have cycles. Those highs and lows can impact your bottom line. Do not be quick to assume your business is a failure when you may actually be in a downward part of a business cycle. Home prices go up and down, and there are always circumstances on a larger scale that impact the industry.

What are your industry's cyclical points? Do you have a plan to address or ride through that cycle? Depending on the industry, it might be necessary to consider getting out while the market is doing well and exiting your business by selling it altogether. I sold my East Coast real estate business prior to the downturn. The timing was good, and I took advantage of the cyclical change I saw coming in my own industry.

It was a moment where I acted, and I benefited financially. Do not let yourself get mired in the process of deciding, leaving you unable to act. When you do so, you put yourself at risk of not being able to grow and thrive professionally. People want to know they are in good hands when they come to you as an expert in your field. If you are not willing to act, then opportunities for doubling your income will be missed. You cannot grow a business if you are not willing to act and take risks to achieve your goals.

No one stood in the winners' circle because they chose not to act. Actions create growth, which is essential to reaching your goals and achieving your dreams.

Throughout this book, I have shared the 8 Success Secrets that made me successful in different industries. Take these as stepping stones to support you in reaching the next level in your industry. While I was primarily focused in real estate, these keys are not limited to that arena.

Service industries are built on your ability to build relationships with people.

Even if you are selling products instead of services, you need to build a level of trust with your clients to keep them coming back and referring others. The 8 Success Secrets that I have outlined here can assist you in building that trust and taking your client relationships to new heights.

As you begin to implement these secrets, it is important to set goals and define the path of where you are taking your business. The 8 Success Secrets are actions that, when applied, can assist you in reaching those goals. I encourage you to act and look for ways to make these 8 Success Secrets part of your business on a daily basis. The results will be incredible as you create your amazing career, achieve financial success, and Double Your Income!

Carol M. Paris – Author Biography

Carol M. Paris has over 40 successful years in residential real estate sales and relocation. Carol has owned property in Hawaii since 1968 and has earned numerous designations which attest to her passion and commitment to being the best in her field.

Carol M. Paris began her real estate career in the Virginia/Washington, D.C. area after twelve corporate moves. The knowledge gained from moving her family and household gives her insight to better help people during stressful relocations. For fourteen years, Carol owned and operated a six-division, full-service real estate company, Carol Paris Brown, Inc. REALTORS® Carol helps relocate many people including employees of small and large companies, such as Gannett Publishing (USA Today), Chevron, Kapiolani Hospital and Kaiser Permanente. Carol M. Paris also works with all branches of the military.

Carol enjoys guest speaking at real estate conventions and meetings, imparting her expertise to other real estate agents in various areas of the industry.

Carol has served as a Governor of the National Association of Realtors® Residential Sales Council. She has achieved additional designations and awards in Hawaii, which includes Top Producer awards at Keller Williams Honolulu for the Honolulu Keller Williams Realty office.

When Carol has spare time she enjoys traveling, dancing, music, and spending time with family and friends.

Real Estate Achievements:
Top 1% of Realtors® Nationwide
Personal Production 1000+ Home Sales
Omega Tau Rho Award – National Association of REALTORS®
REALTOR® Emeritus Status – National Association of REALTORS®
REALTOR® of the Year – Northern Virginia Association of Realtors®
Certified Residential Specialist of the Year – Virginia (Twice)
ABR – Accredited Buyers Representative
CIPS – Certified International Property Specialist
CLHMS – Certified Luxury Home Marketing Specialist
CRB – Certified Residential Broker
CRS – Certified Residential Specialist
GRI – Graduate, Realtor® Institute
MRP – Military Relocation Professional
SRES – Seniors Real Estate Specialist
WCR – Women's Council of Realtors®
Realtor® Associate – Hawaii
Real Estate Broker – Virginia
Accredited Relocation Counselor

Educational Contributions:
Guest Speaker – Pentagon
Guest Speaker – USA Today
Guest Speaker – National Association of REALTORS®
Instructor – Northern Virginia Association of Realtors® Convention
GRI Instructor – Washington, D.C. Board of Realtors®
Instructor – Northern Association of Realtors®

Association Leadership Positions:
Governor – National Association of REALTORS® Residential Sales Council
Director – Virginia Association of Realtors®
President – Virginia CRS Chapter (2 Terms)
Secretary, Treasurer and Vice Chair – Virginia CRS Chapter

Professional and Personal Accomplishments:
Founder/President, Carol Paris Brown, Inc. Realtors®
First Woman elected to the Vienna, Virginia Chapter of Rotary International
Paul Harris Fellow – Rotary International

Member of the Kailua Chamber of Commerce
A long-standing member of STAR (Top Agents in the U.S.)
Hale Ola Windward Spouse Abuse Shelter Volunteer
Hawaii Theatre Star Volunteer
Creator of KailuaOhana.com

Carol M. Paris resides in Kailua, Oahu, Hawaii.

Testimonials

"My wife and I have worked with a variety of real estate agents over the years. Occasionally, an agent would stand out as being above average or even very good. Carol, however, has set a standard that all agents should strive to achieve...Carol is the only agent to ever spend four continuous hours with us in our home, arranging it for the best possible presentation. Carol had all of the snecessary market analyses done at our first meeting. Carol worked open houses for us every single weekend when we asked her to. When we were discouraged, Carol explained the market and provided much needed positive support. The list goes on...it is our honest belief that no other agent could have closed the deal for the sales price Carol got." – M.J.

"Carol worked diligently to determine our housing needs and made sure the homes she located were within our specifications. Her interviewing skills made it easy to develop a search plan quickly... She spent the time to identify qualified candidates (homes) and submitted only those for review. Working with Carol was a unique and refreshing experience." – Z.F.

"I wanted to send a personal message of thanks on behalf of the entire family to both of you for the successful sale of my mother's property. It has indeed been a pleasure to work with you, and I especially appreciate your professionalism and expert advice in helping us navigate our way through this typically stressful and arduous process. The long-distance transaction was a bit of a challenge, as was the market conditions, yet despite that, you succeeded in helping us make this a virtually seamless transaction. If ever you shall require a recommendation for your business, we are happy to oblige. With thanks." – D.L.

"Carol worked very hard on our behalf, even before we arrived on the island...Upon arrival, she provided us with a very detailed orientation to the island. She listened intently to our needs and desires and showed us exactly what we wanted to see each day. She did not waste our time showing us homes that did not fit our criteria. Carol was willing to work long after everyone else had gone home. Had it not been for her insistence that we work past 10 pm on the night we were drafting the contract, we would have lost the sale to two other offers that were submitted the next morning. Thanks to her, we got the home we wanted. She truly takes a personal interest in you and doesn't stop until you are 100% satisfied. Even after the sale, she was there to ensure that things were going well and to tie up any loose ends." – S.L.

"We would like to express our gratitude for the extremely professional service we received by your agent and our newly adopted family member, Ms. Carol M. Paris. Carol's skill, talent, and experience in the real estate market were apparent, and she exceeded all expectations as our agent/advocate. Thank you for meeting our real estate needs and allowing Carol to assist our family in this stressful but exciting transition." – J.C.

"Through the years, we have worked with Carol M. Paris on two separate real estate transactions. In both instances, we encountered unforeseen roadblocks that could have caused us to lose the transaction. We were so lucky to have Carol advising us. She knew exactly what to do to bring the transactions to closing. Carol is the consummate Real Estate Professional. We wouldn't use anyone else!" – J.B.

"Carol is an outstanding Realtor who put forth 110% to sell our home in a timely fashion with persistence and class. She is an exceptional negotiator and multi-tasker." – D.P. & J.P.

"Some of the best advice I ever received was to truly care about people, work hard, and to learn from the experiences of others. Carol Paris' book is an excellent resource for all three!"

– Tom Hopkins, author of *How to Master the Art of Selling* and *When Buyers Say No*

"Carol, you are a sponge for knowledge, and you seem to get more excited about the real estate business every day. You have a wonderful philosophy and an open, warm, charismatic personality. You have become one of the most talented in your real estate field." – Howard Brinton

"Carol Paris will always treat you like family." – Ross M. Brown, R

"Carol,

As we say, first impressions count. Here's why for years, I've counted on you as a friend.

My first impression of you was the way you listen intently to those you admire and respect.

I watch you automatically take in the big picture. That is the whole surroundings, others' moods, body language, and light, quickly combining all with the words that are spoken, and learning from each piece of the communication.

You do this effortlessly, humbly, and with total respect. This is most likely why you are a model student, hence a great teacher/communicator.

Your success has always been inclusive. Understanding and possessing the knowledge of abundance, you are willing give to others. Carol, I believe it's because of this, that all who know you know your heart.

As we have discussed, 'The gift goes to the giver.' And each time we give, the heart grows. Carol, you are all heart. Thanks for all you give."

Keep Smiling,
Jerry Rossi, CDEI
ROSSI Speaks, Inc.

Made in the USA
Columbia, SC
27 January 2018